HAT

7 POWERFUL HABITS FOR BUILDING A
FULFILLING, INTERCONNECTED, RESILIENT LIFE

TIP

J HAROLD BADGER

AR
PRESS

Library of Congress Control Number: 2025905433

Paperback ISBN: 978-1-966283-47-8

Hardback ISBN: 978-1-966283-48-5

Design, Production, and Content Coordination by True Vine Productions, LLC, J Harold Badger, Executive Editor.

Published by American Real Publishing.

Cover design and photograph by Planetary Rag, (licensed by Shutterstock)

Also by Author

Eat to Live: More Than Health & Wellness, Eating
Well Rocks Longevity (2016)
The Secret to Creating Time (2016)
The Power of a Growth Mindset (2023 by Seneca
Badger)
The Grit Factor: Build Courage, Tenacity, Resilience,
and Endurance into Your Breakout Journey (2023 by
Seneca Badger)
Buckle Up: 7 Habits to Harness the Power of
Concentration and Focused Life (April 2025)
Trim Slack: 7 Principles for Cutting Waste, and
Letting Go of What No Longer Serves You (April
2025)
Trail Tight: 7 Secrets for Creating Time, Staying on
Schedule, and Keeping a Tight Life (May 2025).

"Life is hard. It's even harder when you're stupid." ~John Wayne

Dedication

To my rowdy friends, you have been a pillar of strength and an inspiration to everyone who knows you. Your dedication to your work is extraordinary, as you continue to give your all long after many would have stepped back. Your unmatched work ethic has built an incredible life despite challenges and the relentless pursuit of more.

For most of you, there is a wife by your side whom you simply couldn't live without. Her unwavering support has been the bedrock of your journey. You have raised wonderful children who, in turn, have brought you the joy of beautiful grandchildren, even great-grandchildren.

Yet, I know that you, as I have struggled. The desire for more, the need to feel respected and acknowledged, has sometimes overshadowed the abundance that already fills your life. It may have driven some of your loved ones to distance themselves, feeling the strain of your lofty expectations. The disconnect that has arisen is painful, knowing that beneath it all, you are a man with a heart full of love and a spirit that seeks connection and understanding.

You have it all. You are surrounded by a family that loves you deeply, even if it doesn't always feel that way. The recognition you seek and the respect you desire are already there; woven into the fabric of your relationships and the lives you have touched. I am reminding you the love of God, the greatest love of all, envelops you always, offering a peace that transcends all earthly desires.

I pray you can find peace through gratitude for all you have now. Embrace the abundance already yours and more will follow from the love surrounding you and the blessings filling your life.

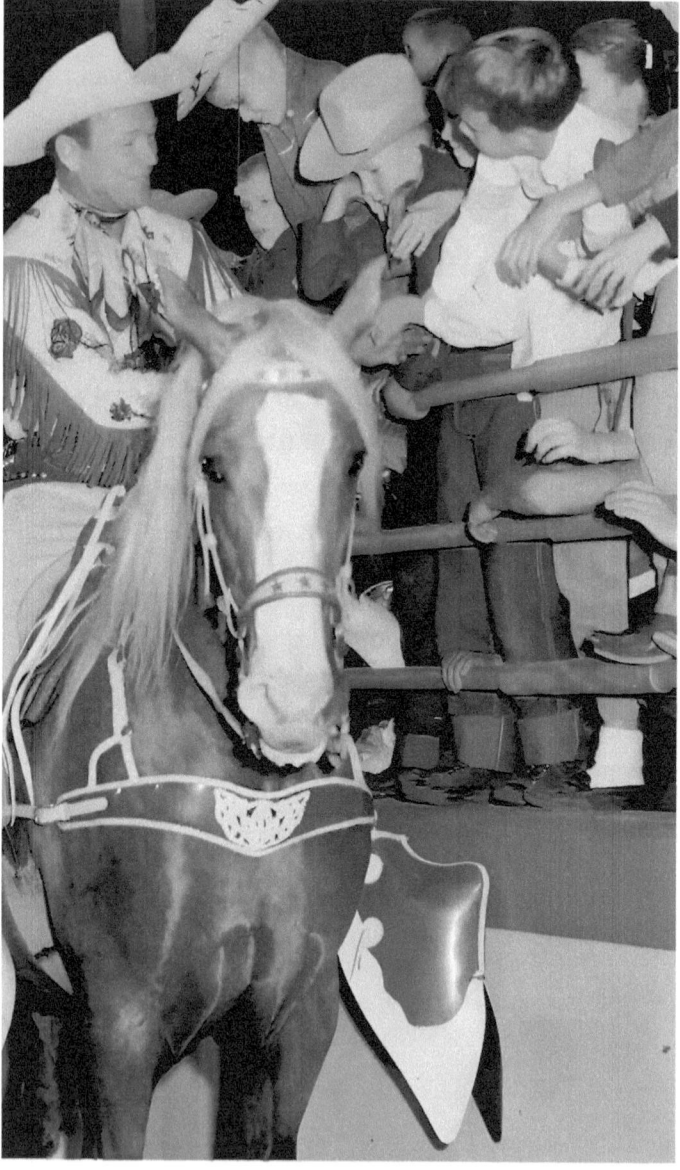

In My Time

"There's a big difference between me and a natural, legitimate working horseman, cowhand, or a world champion rodeo cowboy. I write about them and am grateful to have experienced them and their remarkable grit and resiliency, but those guys are extremely tough—me, not so much." ~the Author

AS I WALK PAST MY 80th year, I find myself reflecting on a journey that, in many ways, has only just begun. It took 24 months to bring this book to life, but the transformation underlying its pages has been quietly unfolding for years. Recently, God has been speaking into my life with a clarity I could not have predicted, altering the path I once thought I knew. This book, Hat Tip: 7 Powerful Habits for Building a Fulfilling, Interconnected,

Resilient Life, is the culmination of that journey—a journey shaped by the realization that, in life, "there are always two plans for your life; yours and God's. I have learned that one will always fail, and that it will be yours. Pray that you fully surrender to this and have time to discover and live it out.

Growing up, the pulse of Western horse culture shaped my life. I still recall the thrill of sitting at the Houston Fat Stock Show in the 1950s when Roy Rogers and his horse Trigger stopped in front of me. That handshake began a lifelong admiration for the Western ethos, which has permeated my writing. While I may not have been a cowboy by trade, my life has been shaped by the rugged resilience, deep faith, and authenticity that characterize those who live it.

My reflections here celebrate these virtues through the stories of people who have embodied them. Some of their stories carry a touch of fable. Yet, each is grounded in a deep-seated reverence for perseverance, integrity, and God's presence. They reflect values that not only molded me but have also guided me to let go of past burdens and embrace a life of gratitude.

Over the past decade, my life has shifted in profound ways. The relationships I've built, the faith I've discovered, and the gratitude I've come to cherish have transformed me. My journey, filled with unexpected twists and remarkable people, led me to a deeper relationship with Jesus and a fuller understanding of grace, love, and stewardship.

This book invites you to join me on this journey.

Each chapter stands alone, offering insights and habits that can be explored independently. Whether you are drawn to themes of resilience, interconnectedness, or the quiet power of gratitude, I hope these pages inspire you to lean into life with faith and humility. I am grateful to have you here to share in this journey, one shaped by a willingness to surrender to God's plan and discover His purpose for each of us.

Jim

J Harold (Jim) Badger
Richmond, Texas

Table of Contents

Introduction

I F THIS BOOK SPEAKS TO a life of gratitude, what does a simple gesture of tipping one's hat have to do with a grateful mindset? It might appear to be a quaint and archaic tradition that we associate with a bygone era or scenes from old Western movies. However, beneath its trivial surface, tipping one's hat carries profound significance akin to expressing gratitude. It's a custom deeply rooted in culture and history, and its essence resonates with the human inclination to push through our natural negative bias and to acknowledge and appreciate the good in others.

Although less common in today's urban environments, tipping one's hat has kept its meaning. It is still a powerful symbol of respect and gratitude, harkening back to when manners and etiquette played a prominent societal role.

We can use biblical examples illuminating this enduring tradition to fully appreciate the connection between a tip of the hat and gratitude.

In the Bible, we encounter instances where individuals express their respect and gratitude through gestures like a hat tip. One such example is found in the story of David and King Saul. After David spared Saul's life when he had the opportunity to take it, Saul acknowledged this act of mercy with gratitude and admiration. He exclaimed, "You are more righteous than I; for you repaid me good, whereas I have repaid you evil" 1 Samuel 24:17. While this might not involve the literal act of tipping a hat, it illustrates the fundamental concept of stepping out of the norm and acknowledging someone's good deed with gratitude and respect, probably, in this case with a slight bow rather than a tip of the hat.

Similarly, in the New Testament, the story of the Good Samaritan exemplifies the essence of gratitude. When the Samaritan came to the aid of the injured traveler, he not only tended to his wounds but also ensured his well-being. This selfless act of kindness and compassion can be seen as a profound expression of gratitude for the gift of helping another human being in need.

In today's fast-paced and increasing digital world, the traditional act of tipping one's hat has evolved. While not everyone wears a hat as a daily attire, the gesture lives on in various forms. In the heart of Texas or small towns throughout the Southwest or the deep South, you might still meet individuals who "tip their hats" to show appreciation for someone's good performance or to pay homage to traditions. Even in urban settings, where the fedoras of Humphrey Bogart are a rarity, the spirit of the hat tip endures.

I had my older son Jason in town from Alamogordo, NM, in the spring of 2018 when I started researching this book. As is our family tradition when he comes into town, my younger son Niko, Jason, and I always find a place and time to go see the 2010 version of "True Grit" a Western film directed by the Coen Brothers, featuring Jeff Bridges as Rooster Cogburn, a tough, grizzled U.S. Marshal with a penchant for whiskey. The story follows 14-year-old Mattie Ross (played by Hailee Steinfeld), who is determined to avenge the murder of her father. The film depicts their perilous journey into Indian Territory, where they are joined by LaBeouf (played by Matt Damon), a Texas Ranger who also seeks Chaney for a separate crime. The trio faces various dangers throughout the journey, developing an unlikely mutual respect.

A pivotal moment in the film occurs to avenge her father's murder by hiring Cogburn to track down and capture the killer, Tom Chaney (played by Josh Brolin). Mattie insists on accompanying Cogburn, proving her resilience and tenacity.

After a tough negotiation, Rooster agrees to Mattie's terms for the bounty hunt. Successfully negotiating with Mattie, he tips his hat to her and says, "Well, by God, girl, that's a Colt's Dragoon! You're no bigger than a corn nubbin; what're you doing with all this pistol?" This line shows his surprise at her preparedness and armament and indirectly compliments her bold spirit and determination. Rooster's hat tip is a pivotal moment where he acknowledges his gratitude for Mattie's fortitude and capability, setting the stage for their mutual respect and the dynamic that follows through the rest of their adventure. Rooster is grateful for her as a partner rather than a mere tagalong. The scene is a subtle yet powerful nod to Mattie's growing influence and importance in the journey, highlighting the film's themes of grit, justice, and the strength of character.

It gave me the idea for the title of this book, the hat tip symbolizing how gratitude shifted Rooster's viewpoint from a negative to a positive. It changed his focus.

The Cambridge Dictionary succinctly defines a hat tip as "the fact of showing gratitude for or approval of something someone has done." While the act may vary from era to place to place, its core meaning remains unchanged: it is a sign of respect and gratitude for another person's positive actions or qualities.

While a hat tip may be an unfamiliar concept to some, expressing gratitude is a practice deeply ingrained in human culture all-be-it, occasionally hidden in the youngest of us; from an early age, we are taught to say "thank you" as an essential expression of appreciation. As a young man, I think back to the times when my mother reminded me that I needed to make it a point to write thank-you notes after receiving birthday presents. As a teenager, I thought this suggestion was an imposition to ignore. This came at my peril as my grandmother threatened to remove me from her favorite grandson's status. As I grew into a broke college student, I realized the vast returns that could be generated from thank-you notes, a thought pattern I am not so gratified by today. Later in business, maturity dragged me kicking and screaming into life as an adult. The gratitude seeds that my mother and grandmother had planted in me helped me develop a sense of well-being from the appreciation for the kindness and generosity of others.

As we navigate the complexities of modern life, the true essence of gratitude, as with me in my early years, can sometimes become obscured by the pursuit of our ambitions and desires. We become so focused on chasing after what we want, on reaching some distant goal, that we forget to savor the present moment. We need to remember to be content with what we have.

How often have you heard people say, "I'll be content when I get this or that," or "I'll be content when I achieve this milestone"? And yet, when those goals are reached, the cycle continues with new aspirations. In this perpetual chase, we risk overlooking the beauty of our current circumstances and the achievements we've already accomplished. We neglect to be grateful for the present moment and our life. The Apostle Paul reminds us of this in Philippians 4:11–12: "….I have learned in whatever situation I am to be content. I know how to be brought low, and I know how to abound. In any and every circumstance, I have learned the secret of facing plenty and hunger, abundance and need."

Essence Of Gratitude

What comes to mind when you think of the word "gratitude"? Do you automatically think of saying thank you when someone opens the door for you? Or do you feel grateful when somebody gives you a birthday gift? While those things come under the gratitude umbrella, this isn't the kind of gratitude that is earth-shattering and life changing. I'm talking about the transformative type of thankfulness that can change your life and give you a new perspective. A mindset that will change your relationship with God, family, friends, and the physical universe as it did for me.

I learned late in life that the real art of being grateful is continually developing an awareness of what you have. While I concentrated on what I didn't have, the Law of Attraction kept providing the "lack of it."

On the other hand, when I began regularly expressing gratitude much later in life, I transitioned from constantly focusing on lack to concentrate on the abundance I have right now.

As discussed later in depth, there are also health benefits to adopting this practice of gratitude. Many studies have shown that gratitude makes people happier and more resilient to life's challenges. One such study, in 2010, found substantial evidence to support the idea that gratitude is associated with increased happiness and life satisfaction. The study also showed that gratitude improved emotional well-being, reduced symptoms of depression, and enhanced individuals' ability to cope with life's challenges.

Gratitude isn't just a fashionable word. Even if you give the idea of gratitude a little more thought than the average person, you may still fail to grasp the importance of being thankful. We hear a lot these days about gratitude –so much so that gratitude is becoming nothing more than just a buzzword with little or no meaning. If being grateful has lost all relevance to you, it's time to look again, return to the drawing board, and redefine the word's meaning. Suppose you only link thankfulness with holidays and gift-giving. In that case, it's time to look again at the entire concept of gratitude.

Discussing the essence of gratitude begs the question, what does it mean to feel grateful? Living a life filled with gratitude means focusing on what you appreciate most. That doesn't mean you must block out any difficulties or problems you face. However, it does mean you can learn how to approach such challenges from a new viewpoint.

Feeling appreciative can soften your heart and soothe your mind. It helps you connect with the things and people around you, large and small that we often take for granted.

The key to a thankful and transformed life is to look at the little things rather than focusing on the big ones.

The Bible has much to say: 1 Thessalonians 5:18: "Give thanks in all circumstances; for this is the will of God in Christ Jesus for you." The Bible encourages us to be thankful in all circumstances, not just when things are going well. Focusing on unimportant things can help cultivate a spirit of gratitude.

Often, the challenges we face can feel entirely overwhelming, and they become the center of our universe. Yet, that's where unhappiness lies. Usually, the most significant problems are those we can do little about, or that take the longest time to put right. Spending all your time focusing on these things can only lead to unhappiness and dissatisfaction.

Expressing gratitude changes your outlook and makes you feel better, even in the face of challenges. Overlook those huge issues you're trying to overcome. Instead, narrow it down to the little blessings you've experienced daily. Something as simple as a sunny day or receiving a card in the mail from a loved one can make you feel grateful. When you're feeling thankful, your whole body responds positively. You feel lighter, warmer, and happier.

Simply put, gratitude helps us to see that not everything is awful all the time. Even in times of trouble, little sparks of light can make you feel better, even if only for a while.

Ancient Philosophy

"Wealth consists not in having great possessions, but in having few wants."
– Epictetus.[2]

The concept of gratitude as a virtue is deeply rooted in human history and has been present across various cultures and civilizations. From ancient philosophical and religious teachings to modern psychological research, gratitude has been recognized as a fundamental human principle with profound implications for individual well-being and social harmony.

In ancient civilizations, expressions of gratitude were often intertwined with religious practices and rituals. In ancient Egypt, for instance, gratitude was directed towards the gods and pharaohs, and various ceremonies and offerings were made to express thankfulness for blessings and protection. Similarly, in ancient Greece, gratitude was a virtue associated with humility and recognizing dependence on the gods and the community.

In Scripture, gratitude is a recurring theme. Gratitude is a way to acknowledge the Lord's blessings and providence. Biblical figures like King David in the Psalms and the Apostle Paul in his letters often express gratitude to God for His mercy, guidance, and deliverance. Ancient philosophers also recognized the importance of gratitude in fostering a virtuous and fulfilling life. For example, in ancient Rome, Cicero highlighted the role of gratitude in cultivating good character and moral excellence. The Stoics, including Marcus Aurelius, emphasized the practice of gratitude as a means of achieving inner tranquility and contentment, irrespective of external circumstances.

Throughout history, cultures worldwide have also celebrated harvest festivals and thanksgiving ceremonies to express gratitude for bountiful harvests and the gifts of nature. These celebrations often involve communal gatherings, feasts, and expressions of gratitude towards the earth and the spirits believed to provide for their sustenance.

In medieval Europe, chivalry was linked to gratitude, with knights and noblemen expected to show appreciation and respect to their lords and patrons. The practice of courtly love also involved expressions of gratitude and devotion between lovers.

Philosophers like David Hume and Immanuel Kant explored gratitude's moral and social dimensions during the Enlightenment. Hume considered gratitude a crucial aspect of human nature. In contrast, Kant linked gratitude to the duty of reciprocity and the categorical imperative of treating others as ends, not merely as a means to an end.

In the modern era, psychology and social science have delved into the study of gratitude and its impact on human well-being. Secular research has shown that cultivating gratitude can improve mental and emotional health, increase life satisfaction, and enhance social relationships. Keeping gratitude journals and expressing thanks to others has gained popularity for enhancing overall happiness and resilience.

In recent years, the science of positive psychology, spearheaded by researchers like Martin Seligman, has focused on gratitude as one of the critical elements of flourishing and well-being. Gratitude interventions have been incorporated into various therapeutic approaches and self-help programs, further underscoring the significance of gratitude in modern secular well-being.

As you can see, gratitude has woven its way through the tapestry of human history, manifesting itself in religious, philosophical, and cultural contexts. From ancient civilizations to contemporary societies, gratitude has remained a timeless virtue that transcends boundaries and enriches human experience. Its enduring importance in promoting individual happiness, fostering social cohesion, and nurturing a sense of interconnectedness underscores the profound impact of gratitude on the human psyche and society.

The Biblical Perspective

It's crucial for you, as it was for me, to recognize that, at this very moment, you possess more than enough reasons to be grateful. While it's entirely valid to have dreams, aspirations, and ambitions, it's equally important to celebrate yourself and your accomplishments, no matter how small they may seem.

Gratitude is the bridge to happiness, and happiness, in turn, fuels gratitude.

Understanding the power of a grateful heart and integrating it into your daily life can transform you profoundly. This transformation is not just about feeling good; it's about attracting more positivity and abundance into your life. This concept aligns with the Law of Attraction, which suggests that shifting your focus toward gratitude will bring more of what you want into reality.

To fully embrace the power of gratitude, we must cultivate and nurture gratitude daily, spiritually, and as human beings in our natural lives. This is often said to be practicing gratitude or cultivating an attitude of gratitude. I address it as developing a grateful mindset. To accomplish this involves shifting your perspective and learning to appreciate the abundance in your life. This book will explore how to create and nurture this mindset, providing practical advice and exercises to help you integrate gratitude into your daily routine. Making gratitude a part of your daily life is essential for reaping its benefits. We will introduce you to practical methods and practices for incorporating gratitude into your daily routine. These techniques are designed to become second nature, transforming gratitude into a habit that naturally enriches your life.

Gratitude isn't confined to personal happiness; it can also improve your relationships with others. In the pages ahead, we'll explore methods for using gratitude to enhance your connections with friends, family, and colleagues. You'll discover how a simple expression of thanks can deepen bonds, resolve conflicts, and foster a more positive and harmonious environment, peace, and joy through a grateful personal relationship with God.

As you delve into the following Chapters, remember that gratitude is a transformative force that can reshape your perspective and, in turn, your life. Embrace it wholeheartedly, and you will find yourself on a path to greater optimism, happiness, and a deep appreciation for the world around you.

The concept of stewardship is also presented in the Bible, which means taking care of and appreciating the blessings and talents God has given us. This includes recognizing and celebrating the skills and achievements we have been blessed with. In the Parable of the Talents (Matthew 25:14-30), Jesus tells a story of servants who were entrusted with different talents, and those who used them wisely were praised. In Philippians 4:11-12 we are also encouraged to find contentment and happiness in our current circumstances while also striving for our goals. Celebrating even small accomplishments can contribute to a sense of joy.

While celebrating accomplishments is essential, humility is also an emphasized virtue. Proverbs 27:2 says, "Let another praise you, and not your own mouth; a stranger, and not your own lips." This verse reminds us to be humble and not boastful, even as we celebrate our achievements.

Finally, the Bible teaches that God has a plan for everyone's life. Jeremiah 29:11 states, "For I know the plans I have for you, declares the Lord, plans for welfare and not for evil, to give you a future and a hope." Celebrating our accomplishments can be seen as acknowledging God's guidance and providence. Celebrating our achievements in the community with others can bring joy and encouragement to those around us, fostering a sense of unity and shared blessings within a community.

Dr. Charles Stanley expresses it from a Christian perspective, "... We often lose our joy as we get side-tracked by life's responsibilities, struggles, and challenges." He says, "...our gratitude should overflow in response to the benefits we receive as children of God. A thankful heart is a defining characteristic of a (godly) person since it's an expression of God's indwelling presence. Even in the Old Testament, the Lord desired gratitude from His people. They didn't have the Bible, so He used a sacrificial system of worship to teach them that He—the holy, sovereign God—was the source of every good thing. They learned to express their gratitude by bringing Him offerings.

Gratitude and happiness are intertwined, each feeding into the other continuously. By embracing gratitude, individuals can cultivate a more optimistic and joyful outlook on life, propelling them toward greater fulfillment and satisfaction. The practices and insights shared in this book aim to empower individuals to embrace gratitude wholeheartedly and unlock its transformative potential. Developing an attitude of gratitude is a journey worth undertaking, leading to a more enriching and fulfilling existence. So, let us take a moment to metaphorically tip our hats to appreciation, acknowledging its profound impact and welcoming its presence into our daily lives.

The Bible encourages us to be grateful for our accomplishments, no matter how small, and to find happiness in recognizing the blessings and talents they have been given. At the same time, humility, contentment, and recognizing God's plan are essential aspects of celebrating oneself from a biblical perspective.

The Grateful Mindset

My experiences led me to believe gratitude has no defining explanation. You will see definitions for gratitude that center around emotions, traits, attitudes, habits, and even morals. Gratitude is complex and dynamic.

As humans, we are wired to pay more attention to adverse events and experiences than positive ones—a phenomenon known as negativity bias. However, by consciously cultivating gratitude, we can counteract this tendency and shift our focus towards the positive aspects of our lives. By actively seeking out and acknowledging the blessings within and around us, we train our brains to perceive the world through gratitude, fostering greater happiness and fulfillment.

The Stoics saw that wanting less correlates to increased gratitude, just as wanting more obliterates it. Psychologists call that hedonic adaptation. They sought to reduce this destructive habit of wanting more; they saw the key to a happy life and relationships. To the Stoics, gratitude is a feeling of appreciation and a way of life. It is recognition that we are part of a larger whole and that everything we have is a gift for which we should be grateful. By cultivating a sense of gratitude, we can learn to appreciate the present moment and find joy in the simple things in life.

For me, gratitude is a skill. When you cultivate the talent of gratitude, your life will dramatically transform.

You may read that gratitude is strongly connected to moods and emotions. Emotion is a definite personal experience based on your belief regarding an event. In that regard, you can feel gratitude based on your belief that something worthwhile has happened.

On the other hand, something I call transformative gratitude is more than an emotion. It is a mindset that becomes cause over your life, not the effect of a life event. Transformative gratitude is a profound and powerful perspective that transcends mere emotion; it is a way of thinking that can actively shape the course of your life. Unlike the feeling of gratitude, which often arises as a reaction to specific life events or circumstances, transformative gratitude is proactive and intentional. It involves consciously adopting gratitude as a guiding principle, regardless of external circumstances.

Gratitude, as described in the Bible, is a powerful mindset that influences the course of your life, shaping your perspective, decisions, and actions. Instead of being a mere effect of circumstances, gratitude becomes a cause that impacts your life and those around you.

The Apostle Paul emphasizes in 1Thessalonias 5:16-18 the transformative power of gratitude.

Giving thanks in all circumstances depends not on the nature of the situation but on a heart aligned with God's will. Gratitude, paired with continual prayer and joy, reflects a life rooted in faith. Paul's words remind us of that cultivating gratitude in every season is both a choice and a reflection of our trust in God's sovereignty and goodness.

A grateful mindset empowers individuals to live with purpose and joy, positively impacting their lives and the lives of those around them.

In this way, gratitude becomes a cause over your life, not merely an effect. Instead of waiting for positive experiences or blessings to trigger feelings of thankfulness, individuals who embrace this mindset make gratitude a foundational aspect of their daily lives. They recognize that gratitude is not solely dependent on external factors but is an internal state of mind that can be cultivated and nurtured.

Transformative gratitude empowers individuals to take control of their well-being by actively being thankful for the big and small blessings surrounding them. It becomes a way of life, a compass that guides you toward a more fulfilling and meaningful existence—cherishing the insignificant things.

Life is full of small things that you can easily take for granted. These unimportant things can help you appreciate your life a lot more. Become more aware of nature. For example, when you see a beautiful butterfly, be grateful that nature can bring you these lovely things.

What about the food that appears on your table every day? What about the fact that you have air to breathe and the energy to do what you need and want to do? Yes, these things are simple, but when you acknowledge and appreciate them, you will be even happier with your life.

Psycology of Gratitude

> "When I started counting my blessings,
> that's when my whole life turned around."
> —**Willie Nelson**[3]

THE PSYCHOLOGICAL BENEFITS OF GRATITUDE are well-known and have been extensively studied. An early study in 2003 explored how practicing gratitude by counting blessings daily can increase well-being and positive emotions. This study and others show that gratitude brings psychological benefits that can significantly enhance well-being.

The Apostle Paul wrote in Philippians 4:6-7, "Do not be anxious about anything, but in every situation, by prayer and supplication, with thanksgiving, your requests to be known to God. And the peace of God, which transcends all understanding, will guard your hearts and your minds...." Paul is saying that expressing gratitude and turning to God in prayer is associated with receiving His peace, which can alleviate anxiety and depressive feelings. This profound connection between gratitude and inner peace from a personal relationship with Jesus underscores gratitude's powerful impact on our mental and emotional well-being.

Mitigating the Cycle of Stress and Depression

Adopting a gratitude mindset can break the cycle of stress, depression, and their physical and emotional repercussions.

Depression, a silent and pervasive affliction, affects a sizable portion of the global population. A quarter of individuals will grapple with a mental health problem at some point in their lifetime. Among these conditions, depression stands out as one of the most prevalent and debilitating.

Depression, with its multifaceted nature, has both neurochemical and psychological foundations. Gratitude, as an active and spiritual practice, holds the potential to positively impact both aspects, offering us a complementary means to navigate the complex terrain of depression.

The transformation initiated by gratitude begins with a shift in attention. When you actively practice gratitude, your focus naturally transitions from dwelling on problems to actively seeking solutions.

This subtle yet profound change in perspective has significant implications for mental health. It initiates a cascade of neurochemical events in the brain that contribute to enhanced emotional well-being.

Key neurotransmitters, such as oxytocin, dopamine, and serotonin, play pivotal roles in regulating mood and emotions. Oxytocin, often called the "love hormone," fosters feelings of trust and connection with others. Dopamine is associated with pleasure and reward, while serotonin influences feelings of happiness and contentment. Practicing gratitude triggers the release of these "feel-good" chemicals, promoting a sense of motivation and reducing apathy. This shift is particularly significant for individuals grappling with depression, as it helps weaken the grip of the condition on their lives.

Gratitude extends its influence beyond the surface, reaching into the intricate neurochemical interactions underlying depression. One of its remarkable effects is the reduction of stress hormones and the modulation of the autonomic nervous system. Stress, a pervasive component of depressive experiences, often exacerbates symptoms and hinders recovery. By adopting a mindset of gratitude, individuals can mitigate the impact of stress, leading to a decrease in the unwanted physical and emotional manifestations associated with depression.

Moreover, gratitude's impact extends to the prefrontal cortex, a brain region responsible for managing negative emotions, including shame and guilt. Increased neural activity in this region can result in a more positive outlook and heightened happiness among individuals struggling with depression. This rewiring of the brain's response to negativity is a testament to gratitude's transformative potential.

The most astonishing facet of gratitude's influence on depression is its capacity to reshape the neural structures of the brain Itself. This neural plasticity, as it's known, contributes to increased contentment and happiness among individuals battling depression. As they cultivate a habit of appreciating others and feeling grateful, the brain releases higher levels of dopamine and serotonin, often called the "brain's feel-good hormones." These neurochemical changes, in turn, contribute to regulating the immune system's function, creating a healthier internal environment that is more conducive to recovery.

While the Bible does not explicitly mention the term "depression" as a modern psychological condition, it contains verses and principles that offer valuable insights into the potential of gratitude to alleviate emotional distress and foster inner peace.

A passage we rely on continuously is this book, 1 Thessalonians 5:13-18, underscores the transformative power of gratitude as a spiritual practice. By giving thanks in every situation, even amidst challenges, we align ourselves with God's will and open our hearts to His peace and comfort. Gratitude becomes a pathway to joy and serenity, reminding us that God's presence is with us in all circumstances.

This timeless verse encapsulates the essence of gratitude as a transformative practice. It encourages individuals to transcend anxiety and emotional turmoil by turning to prayer and petition, infused with thanksgiving. The act of gratitude is intertwined with seeking divine intervention, fostering a sense of trust in God's plan, and acknowledging His blessings. While not explicitly addressing depression, this principle of gratitude, faith in God, and seeking His guidance during challenging times holds profound implications for emotional well-being.

Reducing depression through gratitude is profound and multifaceted. It involves a shift in perspective, a cascade of neurochemical changes, and a rewiring of the brain's response to negativity. While the Bible may not speak directly to modern psychological conditions, it brings to bear biblical truths that dictate adopting a gratitude mindset and its ability to alleviate emotional distress and foster inner peace.

The Ubiquity of Stress in Modern Life

Stress has become an ever-present companion in modern life's fast-paced and demanding world. From the pressures of demanding jobs to the constant juggling required in our families, it's no surprise that many people find it challenging to cope with stress effectively. However, the profound relationship between stress and gratitude, as revealed through scientific studies, holds valuable insights, and resonates with biblical teachings.

Studies examining the connection between stress and gratitude have unveiled fascinating results. Participants who actively practiced gratitude demonstrated a substantial reduction in their stress hormone levels, particularly cortisol.

Moreover, they exhibited greater resilience when faced with negative experiences and emotional setbacks. These findings emphasize the transformative potential of gratitude in helping individuals manage and mitigate the detrimental effects of stress.

The Bible, a timeless source of wisdom and guidance, offers profound insights into the practice of gratitude and its role in reducing stress. One foundational biblical principle that aligns with appreciation is Colossians 3:15: "And let the peace of Christ rule in your hearts, to which indeed you were called in one body. And be thankful." This verse highlights the connection between gratitude and the peace that comes from Christ, encouraging us to cultivate thankfulness as an integral part of our lives.

By embracing gratitude, we allow the peace of Christ to guide our hearts, even amidst challenges and uncertainties. Recognizing and appreciating God's blessings, big and small, helps us shift our focus from stress to trust, fostering a sense of calm and assurance rooted in His unwavering love and provision.

Gratitude equips us with the tools to manage stress more effectively by encouraging us to appreciate and acknowledge the small positives in life. This practice gradually rewires our brains, enabling us to confront life's challenges with heightened awareness and a more constructive perception.

It is crucial to recognize that stress, in its various forms, is a natural bodily response to change, whether perceived as positive (eustress) or negative (distress). Gratitude plays a pivotal role in this context. By actively practicing gratitude (adopting a gratitude mindset), we release stress hormones and boost positive emotions, such as happiness.

Adopting a gratitude mindset daily and consistently expressing gratitude can reduce the negative emotions that often accompany stress, effectively detoxing our bodies and minds. This aligns with the biblical principle of renewing our minds and transforming our hearts. Romans 12:2 states, "Do not be confirmed to this world, but be transformed by the renewal of your mind, that by testing you may discern what is the will of God, what is good and acceptable and perfect." The practice of gratitude is a powerful tool for renewing our minds and aligning our thoughts with God's will, enabling us to navigate the challenges of stress with grace and resilience.

While gratitude alone may not offer immediate relief from acute stress, nor does it promise an overnight transformation of our emotional state, it is a valuable tool to help us accept our feelings and work towards making them more manageable. With time and practice, we can develop the skills to combat and cope with stress more effectively, leading to a healthier mental and emotional state. With its timeless wisdom, the Bible reinforces the importance of gratitude as a transformative practice that can bring us peace, joy, and strength, even amid life's most demanding moments.

Greater Self-Esteem

Low self-esteem, a pervasive issue affecting individuals worldwide, has far-reaching consequences that touch every aspect of one's life. It often serves as the breeding ground for other mental health problems, such as depression and anxiety, which can be debilitating and isolating. However, a powerful antidote to low self-esteem has been consistently affirmed through more than a few studies; gratitude.

Gratitude can transform individuals, elevating their self-esteem and positively impacting their interactions.

Over the last few years, I have gradually retired from active business life and increased my involvement in faith-based activities. During this time, I have also increased my writing, among other projects, rewriting and transforming my secular writings of 2015, this being one of them, adding significant faith-based content and experiences. I met and developed solid relationships with many god-fearing men and women during that time.

David Mertins is one of them. He is a retired marketing executive known for his unwavering faith and practice of gratitude, and he is someone I can call a close friend and confidant. As an elder in our local Bible church, he embodies the teachings of compassion and gratefulness. His daily life is a testament to those values. Being involved with David personally and in discipleship missions, I have had the opportunity to observe him at many contrasting times of the day. David has become an ongoing inspiration for this book. David rises early daily to start his day with prayer and meditation. He thanks the Lord for the gift of a new day, the breath in his lungs, and the blessings surrounding him. He prepares to face the world and its challenges with a grateful heart.

One way David expresses gratitude is through his interactions with people. Whether it is a friendly neighbor, a cashier at the grocery store, or a fellow church member, David tries to express his gratitude.

One evening, David cornered me in the kitchen at a dinner gathering at my house. He began talking about a review he had just completed in one of my recent books. Instead of simply saying, "Good job,"

David took a moment to express his gratitude in two meaningful ways. First, he congratulated me with genuine enthusiasm. He said, "Jim, I want to congratulate you on the outstanding work you did on your (newest) book. Your obvious hard work in bringing the message of the book into a clear view and highlighting the work of others on the subject with equal enthusiasm and credit. I am grateful for the opportunity to read it."

Secondly, David took the time to listen to my experiences and challenges in developing the manuscript. He empathized with my struggles. "I know it wasn't easy, Jim, though it appears to me that your perseverance paid off. Your success is a testament to your hard work and faith."

I have to say, I felt deeply appreciated by David's heartfelt words. I expected a simple acknowledgment, but his full-throated expressions of gratitude touched my heart and boosted my confidence in a way I hadn't anticipated.

David continued to practice gratitude in many ways throughout the evening, always seeking opportunities to uplift and encourage the other guests. Whether through a smile, a kind word, or a helping hand. He and his wife remained the last to leave, asking if they could help clean up, making it easy for my wife. They certainly made her feel valued and appreciated.

As an elder in a Bible church in Richmond, Texas, David's influence extends beyond his immediate community. His life of gratitude and his commitment to living out the teachings of the Bible inspire others to do the same.

This transformative journey aligns with biblical teachings, shedding light on the profound connection between gratitude and a healthy self-image.

When we cultivate a habit of gratitude by adopting a gratitude mindset, we experience an internal shift and radiate kindness and friendliness towards others. Grateful individuals tend to naturally extend their appreciation to those around them, fostering an atmosphere of warmth and positivity.

The Bible encourages such behavior in Colossians 3:12: "Put on then, as God's chosen ones, holy and beloved, compassionate hearts, kindness, humility, meekness, and patience." Gratitude nurtures these virtues, making individuals more compassionate, kind, and approachable, attracting positive people and support.

Moreover, gratitude enhances one's ability to recognize acts of kindness in others. Accepting kindness can be challenging for individuals struggling with low self-esteem, often accompanied by suspicion and doubt. They may believe that others have ulterior motives or that they are unworthy of such gestures. However, someone who regularly practices gratitude is more likely to accept acts of kindness at face value, believing themselves deserving of such benevolence. This transformation aligns with the biblical principle in Matthew 7:11: "If you then, who are evil, know how to give good gifts to our children, how much more will your Father who is in heaven give good things to those who ask him!" Gratitude opens our hearts to receive the good gifts bestowed upon us by God and others.

The act of shifting to a gratitude mindset shapes an individual's self-image. Individuals naturally start feeling better about themselves by positively thinking and appreciating others and their actions. This process aligns with biblical teachings that emphasize the importance of positive self-perception. Psalm 139:14 says, "I praise you because I am fearfully and wonderfully made; wonderful are your works, my soul knows it well." Gratitude allows individuals to recognize their inherent worth and the beauty of their uniqueness, leading to a more positive self-image.

Furthermore, the positive impact of gratitude is not confined to individuals who have adopted it. Those receiving gratitude also experience its uplifting effects, creating a harmonious cycle of positivity that benefits everyone involved. This principle resonates with Proverbs 11:25: "Whoever brings blessings will be enriched, and one who waters will himself be watered." Gratitude refreshes the spirits of both the giver and the receiver, fostering an atmosphere of goodwill and mutual support.

Wrapping it up, gratitude is a transformative force that significantly enhances psychological well-being, including self-esteem, reducing depression and stress, fostering positive relationships, and adopting a gratitude mindset. Besides improving self-image, gratitude offers a myriad of benefits that are accessible to anyone who wants to be willing. Embracing gratitude is a psychological and spiritual endeavor, aligning with biblical principles that encourage kindness and humility and recognizing our intrinsic worth as creations of a loving and generous God.

Living in abundance

> *"The faultfinder will find faults even in paradise. Love your life, poor as it is. You may perhaps have some pleasant, thrilling, glorious hours, even in a poor house."*
> *~Henry David Thoreau.*[4]

THE OPPOSITE OF GRATITUDE IS focusing on things you do not have in your life. So many people concentrate on lack and end up living a miserable life. If you keep focusing on lack, then you will receive more lack. People never understand this, but it is how the Law of Attraction works, and you cannot get around this life law.

While the Bible does not explicitly mention the Law of Attraction as it is understood in contemporary terms, some biblical principles and verses can be related to this concept. Think about things this way

– if you are always thinking about the things you don't have, this will not make you happy, right?

Aligning Beliefs with Desired Outcomes

The Law of Attraction is a popular concept in modern self-help literature and personal development, often associated with the idea that thoughts and beliefs can influence one's reality and bring about desired outcomes. The Bible speaks to this in Proverbs 23:7: "As a man thinks in his heart, so is he" (KJV). This verse suggests that one's thoughts and beliefs can shape their reality. It aligns with the idea that our thoughts can influence our actions and outcomes.

This is echoed in Galatians 6:7: "Do not be deceived: God cannot be mocked. for whatever one sows, that will he also reap." This verse implies that the consequences of one's actions and thoughts will manifest in one's life, echoing the Law of Attraction's idea that like attracts like.

While these verses may seem to have some parallels with the Law of Attraction, it is essential to recognize that the biblical perspective is rooted in faith in God and aligning one's thoughts and desires with God's will. The focus is not solely on personal gain but on spiritual growth.

There is much discussion about the Law of Attraction. However, a simple explanation, which Scripture supports, is that what you focus on will attract or manifest in your life. People who continuously moan and complain usually find more things to whine about. Have you ever wondered why this is the case? Well, the Law of Attraction gives these people what they want. The complainers' words are returned by providing more negative things to complain about.

So, what does Jesus say? "But what comes out of the mouth, proceeds from the heart, and this defiles a person. For out of the heart come evil thoughts, murder, adultery, sexual immorality, theft, false witness, slander." Mathew 15:18-19. This passage highlights that negativity originates within the heart and can manifest through complaining and poisonous speech.

The reverse is to be grateful for the things you already have. When you do this, you create feelings of abundance. You are speaking positively, which will be responded to by sending more.

By being grateful for what you have, you are focusing your thoughts and setting yourself up to manifest even more things that do not make you happy. You have already learned that gratitude is a potent emotion. When you express it, you generate positive energy that will enable you to manifest more.

The Role of Gratitude in Gaining Abundance

Some people need help understanding the link between gratitude and abundance. I have discovered that the positive energy you create from appreciation will help you align yourself to manifest abundance.

To begin with, gratitude and its relationship with abundance is a recurring theme in the Bible. The Bible guides how gratitude can lead to abundance in material blessings and spiritual fulfillment. One of the fundamental teachings of the Bible is that a grateful heart paves the way for abundance. Psalm 100:4 (NIV) encourages us to approach God with thanksgiving: "Enter his gates with thanksgiving and his courts with praise; give thanks to him and praise his name." This verse suggests gratitude opens the door to God's presence and blessings.

While the Bible speaks of material abundance, it emphasizes spiritual abundance more. Jesus said in John 10:10: "I came that they may have life and have it abundantly." Gratitude for the gift of eternal life through Jesus Christ is the foundation of true abundance in the biblical context.

You will see that as you adopt a gratitude mindset, your life will change for the better and manifest more. Each time you express gratitude; you send strong signals to your subconscious mind. Your subconscious is powerful and will quickly recognize that you appreciate having things in your life.

So, you have two mighty forces that will work for you here. In the secular world, the Law of Attraction responds to the vibrations (thoughts and feelings) you send out when you are grateful for what you have in your life.

And then there is gratitude, which opens the door to God's presence and blessings and fosters contentment with what already exists in one's life.

If you think negatively about life, then you will never experience abundance. The two things just don't fit together. If you want an abundance in your life, you must transform to positive thinking and being grateful for what you have now and what you see around you is a great way to do that.

As you develop your gratitude mindset, you will see remarkable changes in your life. These can be changes in your career or business life, health and well-being, feelings and actions, and social connections.

All it takes to see improvements in your life like this is to stop complaining about what you don't have and appreciate what you do have. This significant positive change will set you on the path to abundance.

Commit to seeing your blessings as much more important than your problems. This will make you much happier and develop a more positive outlook. In time, you will believe that there are no problems you cannot overcome, and that no hardship will make you think negatively about your life.

We all have positive energy that we can tap into when needed. Most people find this hard to accept, but it is true. You are the result of your previous thoughts. If you had negative thoughts in your life up until now, then what you have around you now results from this.

The Universe will always provide abundance. It is around you today and will continue to be there forever. You need to stop focusing on those small negative things in your life that most people seem to concentrate on. Getting all stressed out about taking out the trash is not the way to go, but so many people think like this.

So, if you have negative feelings about having to take out the trash, think about all the food you ate and the things you have that resulted in the trash building up. Wrappers from food items and other things you take for granted are all in the trash can.

This may seem ridiculous, but it is a significant first step toward gratitude and abundance. We all have limiting beliefs that define us and what we have. As a child, you learned that "money doesn't grow on trees," and this has led to you not having enough money in your life.

Limiting beliefs can be changed, and starting to be genuinely grateful for your money now is a step in the right direction. Being thankful for this money, no matter how small, tells the Universe that you want more of it. It also lets your subconscious mind know that money makes you happy.

So, in the journey towards abundance, gratitude stands as a guiding light, illuminating the path to a more fulfilling and prosperous life. As we've explored the insights of famous individuals, biblical verses, and timeless quotes, it becomes evident that gratitude is not merely a sentiment but a transformative force.

By choosing gratitude, we align ourselves with the universe's abundant offerings, inviting positivity and fulfillment into our lives. We break free from limiting beliefs, embrace the present moment, and cultivate a grateful mindset that attracts abundance.

As we reflect on Melody Beattie's words, "Gratitude turns what we have into enough and more. It turns denial into acceptance, chaos into order, confusion into clarity... it makes sense of our past, brings peace for today, and creates a vision for tomorrow," remember that gratitude is not just a practice; it's a gateway to the abundance that awaits you. Embrace it with an open heart and watch your life flourish in ways you never thought possible.

Gratitude & Physiology

> *"Cowboys don't sleep they just wait."* ~*The Author*

RATITUDE IS A POWERFUL EMOTION that enriches our inner world and has profound physical effects on the human body. This Chapter delves into the intricate relationship between gratitude and its remarkable impact on physical well-being. We will explore four critical physical effects of gratitude, supported by medical research, and examine what the Bible says about these effects, sharing some of my experiences that have drastically changed my physical being.

The Elusive Quest for Rest

For as long as I can remember, sleep eluded me. Throughout my professional life and even into retirement, I tossed and turned, my mind racing with thoughts of what I hadn't accomplished that day and what I needed to achieve tomorrow. My ambition drove me to the heights of my working life but robbed me of the peaceful rest I desperately needed. Each night, the weight of unfulfilled tasks and endless to-do lists pressed on me, ensuring that sleep was fleeting and restless.

Desperate for relief, I tried countless strategies to quiet my mind and find restful sleep. I tried everything from counting sheep to playing soothing music, but nothing worked. One well-meaning friend suggested getting up and writing down my thoughts to rid the brain of nagging worries. Dutifully, I kept a notebook and pen by my bedside, and for weeks, I scribbled down my anxieties and plans in the middle of the night. But instead of bringing peace, this exercise only amplified my thoughts, giving them more power over my restless mind.

It wasn't until I began researching for this book that things started to change.

Well into my effort, I started experiencing a sense of gratitude, a shift that would prove to be life changing. I began experiencing solace in the simple things—a sunrise reflecting on the creek behind my house as seen through the window from my writing desk, the sound of my favorite dog Julia's steps as she worked her way up the metal spiral staircase to my office to check on me, and the steadfast love of my family and friends. This feeling of appreciation began to permeate my daily life, and slowly but surely, my nights started to change.

To be clear, developing a lasting sense of gratitude and the mindset to go with it was not an overnight transformation. It required a conscious effort and still does. Each morning, I begin each day by reflecting on a few things I am grateful for. At first, this exercise felt forced and trivial. But over time, it became a cherished ritual that set a positive tone for my day. I rise at 4:30 am, dress for the day, fix a cup of my beloved mushroom coffee, grab my copy of Oswald Chambers's "My Utmost for His Highest... .", the week's copy of the "Epoch Times" and head to my library, reflecting on the blessings I have rather than the tasks left undone from the day before.

During this quiet time, I also find guidance and comfort in scripture, which helps reinforce my new perspective.

Growing Gratitude, Deepening Faith

As my gratitude mindset has grown, so has my relationship with Jesus. I began to understand the peace that comes from trusting in Him and His plan for my life. Jesus' words in Matthew 11:28-30 spoke to my weary soul: "Come to me, all who labor and are heavy laden, and I will give you rest. Take my yoke upon you, and learn from me, for I am gentle and lowly in heart, and you will find rest for your souls. For my yoke is easy, and my burden is light."

These words became a balm for my anxious mind. I let go of the need to control every aspect of my life and instead placed my trust in God's plan. The more I leaned into my faith, the more I experienced a profound sense of peace. This spiritual surrender allowed me to release the worries that had kept me awake for years.

As I continued to explore the Bible, I discovered that caring for our bodies, including getting adequate sleep, is not just wise but a biblical responsibility. Psalm 127:2 states, "In vain you rise early and stay up late, toiling for food to eat—for he grants sleep to those he loves." This verse was a powerful reminder that rest is a gift from God that I had neglected for far too long. I realized that by depriving myself of sleep, I was not honoring the body God had given me.

Furthermore, 1 Corinthians 6:19-20 emphasizes the importance of honoring God with our bodies: "Do you not know that your bodies are temples of the Holy Spirit, who is in you, whom you have received from God? You are not your own; you were bought at a price. Therefore, honor God with your bodies." This realization brought a new commitment to my quest for healthy sleep. I began to see sleep not as a luxury but as a necessary act of stewardship.

Nightly Battles, Spiritual Triumphs

With a heart of gratitude and a newfound relationship with Jesus, I have embarked on a journey toward a peaceful sleep. It wasn't always easy, and there were nights when old habits crept back in. But each time, I reminded myself of my progress and the spiritual truths I had learned.

I developed a bedtime routine that included prayer and reflection. I would thank God for the day's blessings and surrender my worries to Him. This practice not only calmed my mind but also deepened my faith. I also made practical changes, such as creating a restful sleep environment and setting a consistent sleep schedule.

Over time, these efforts bore fruit. I began to experience the kind of restful sleep that had once seemed impossible. I woke up feeling refreshed and rejuvenated, ready to face the day with a heart full of gratitude. The restless nights that had plagued me for so long became a distant memory.

Sleep is an essential aspect of our lives that often gets overlooked in our hectic and demanding world. Quite a few people struggle with sleep-related issues, from insomnia to restless nights filled with tossing and turning. The quest for a good night's sleep has led to various remedies and techniques. Still, one underrated and highly effective approach involves living a grateful life. Acknowledging and appreciating the positive aspects of life, no matter how big or small. It consists in recognizing and being thankful for our blessings, experiences, and people. This simple yet profound mindset shift can impact our sleep quality.

One of the primary ways in which a gratitude mindset contributes to better sleep is through stress reduction. Stress and anxiety are common culprits behind sleep disturbances, making it challenging to fall asleep or stay asleep throughout the night. In the last Chapter, we discussed how gratitude has been shown to reduce stress by shifting our focus away from worries and negative thoughts and redirecting it toward positive aspects of our lives. When we practice gratitude, our brains release dopamine and serotonin, neurotransmitters associated with happiness and relaxation. These neurochemical changes can help calm the nervous system, making it easier to unwind and sleep peacefully. By consistently practicing gratitude, individuals can lower their stress levels and create a more conducive environment for restful sleep.

Anchoring Bedtime Positivity

Another way gratitude contributes to better sleep is by creating positive sleep associations. When we associate our sleep environment and bedtime routines with positive emotions, it becomes easier to transition into a restful state of mind.

For instance, expressing gratitude before bedtime can involve reflecting on the good things that happened during the day or writing them down in a gratitude journal. Doing these anchors our bedtime routine to positive thoughts and feelings. Over time, our brain associates preparing for sleep with gratitude, making relaxing and falling asleep easier as our minds naturally shift towards positive thoughts.

Gratitude also helps us gain perspective on our problems and challenges, which can be especially beneficial for those who have insomnia or other sleep disorders. When we develop a gratitude mindset, we realize our problems may not be as impossible as they initially seemed. This perspective shift can reduce the racing thoughts and worries that often plague those with sleep difficulties, making it easier to fall asleep peacefully.

Additionally, gratitude can help us reframe negative thoughts into more positive ones. Instead of ruminating on past mistakes or worrying about the future, we learn to appreciate the present moment and focus on what we have rather than what we lack. This shift in perspective can be a meaningful change for improving sleep quality. Though not new theories, from my experience, I have found several practical ways to cultivate better sleep. They are:

Express Gratitude Before Bed: As part of your bedtime routine, take a moment to reflect on the positive aspects of your day and express gratitude for them. This can be done through silent meditation, prayer, or simply mentally listing why you are thankful.

Praying for a peaceful sleep: Pray for peaceful sleep and mindfulness techniques, such as deep breathing can help you stay in the present moment and reduce racing thoughts that can interfere with sleep. Combining mindfulness with grateful prayer can be particularly effective in promoting better sleep.

Limit Exposure to Negative Media: Consuming negative or distressing news before bed can increase stress and anxiety, making sleeping harder. Instead, opt for more positive and uplifting content in the evening to set the stage for a peaceful night's sleep.

For me, gratitude cannot be underestimated in improving sleep quality. I find myself sleeping like a baby by embracing a gratitude mindset, creating positive sleep associations, getting perspective on problems, and reframing negative thoughts.

A Decade of Resilience: My Cancer Journey

Our immune system is our body's first line of defense against various illnesses, including viral infections. Gratitude has been shown to bolster the immune system, offering protection against diseases, and aiding in quicker recovery. As a cancer patient who has been beating back metastatic prostate cancer for ten years, I have found that a grateful mindset, combined with nutrition, and exercise, plays a significant role in my journey.

Studies have shown that regular gratitude practice by adopting a grateful mindset can increase the production of immunoglobulin A. This essential antibody plays a crucial role in the immune response. Additionally, by activating the parasympathetic nervous system, gratitude does more than soothe the mind; it directly counteracts the detrimental effects of stress on the immune system. This activation promotes a state of calm and recovery, which is crucial for maintaining physical health. It bolsters self-esteem and motivation, encouraging healthier behaviors vital for longevity and resilience. This includes regular exercise and diligent health monitoring—essential for combatting illness and fostering an environment where healing can flourish.

While gratitude may not cure severe diseases like cancer, it contributes to overall physiological well-being by reducing stress levels. Adopting a grateful mindset has helped me manage the acute stress and worry that goes with the disease, supporting my immune system in the process. It has not only enhanced my ability to cope with the challenges of cancer but has empowered me to sustain a rigorous exercise regimen and commit to a nutritious diet. These efforts are critical in my ongoing fight against the disease, illustrating how a grateful heart can lead to a healthier body. Thus, the thread of gratitude weaves through each aspect of life, reinforcing that a thankful spirit is integral to enduring health and wellness.

Conversely, when gratitude isn't a primary focus in my thoughts daily, I notice a definite shift in my overall well-being. It's as though the light dims, making the burdens of life feel heavier and more daunting. Recognizing and embracing gratitude, especially for God's favor, which keeps me thriving at eighty years old, reinforces my belief that God has not finished His work in me yet. This conviction brings a unique strength and perspective, through my battle with cancer.

Lessons from Pain: Finding Wisdom in Suffering

Dealing with chronic pain for a decade, I have concluded that pain is a complex and multifaceted experience that often signals an underlying issue in the body. In my case, rheumatoid arthritis was a result of early decades of irresponsible (and stupid) thinking that I was invincible, on horseback, in the air, and climbing places that should be left to those who knew what they were doing.

One of the primary culprits behind aches and pains is inflammation. Inflammation is the body's natural response to injury, infection, or harmful stimuli. When tissues are damaged or threatened, the immune system springs into action, releasing chemicals that cause blood vessels to leak fluid into the tissues, activating inflammatory pathways leading to swelling. This involves the release of various molecules, including cytokines and chemokines, which orchestrate the inflammatory response.

While inflammation is crucial for healing, chronic inflammation can lead to persistent pain and other health issues. Conditions such as arthritis, tendonitis, and certain autoimmune diseases are often linked to chronic inflammation, perpetuating the cycle of pain.

Gratitude, a profound sense of thankfulness and appreciation, has been extensively studied for its positive effects on mental and physical health. One of the remarkable benefits of gratitude is its ability to influence the immune system and reduce inflammation. Research has shown that individuals who regularly practice gratitude experience lower inflammatory markers in their blood. This suggests that gratitude can help modulate the immune response, promoting a healthier inflammatory profile. It involves the interaction between the brain and the immune system. Gratitude activates the brain's reward pathways, releasing neurotransmitters such as dopamine and serotonin. These chemicals not only enhance mood but also have anti-inflammatory properties. Additionally, gratitude stimulates the production of endogenous opioids, natural pain-relieving substances produced by the body. This analgesic effect can reduce the perception of pain and increase pain.

Scripture offers profound insights into the role of gratitude in enduring pain and finding strength. In 2 Corinthians 12:9-10, the Apostle Paul writes: "But he said to me, 'My grace is sufficient for you, for my power is made perfect in weakness.' Therefore, I will boast even more gladly of my weaknesses so that the power of Christ may rest on me... For the sake of Christ, then, I am content with weakness, insults, hardships, persecutions, and calamities. For when I am weak, then I am strong." These verses highlight the transformative power of gratitude, even while suffering. Paul's message emphasizes that appreciation for God's grace can provide strength and resilience in times of weakness. By surrendering to a personal relationship with Jesus and acknowledging and appreciating the support and love of God, I have found the fortitude to endure physical pain. This spiritual perspective aligns with modern scientific findings, demonstrating that gratitude can enhance pain tolerance and reduce the emotional burden of suffering. This is a powerful reminder that even amid pain, there is hope and strength to be found in adopting a grateful mindset.

Gratitude is a powerful force that extends beyond emotional well-being to influence physical health. By modulating the immune response and reducing inflammation, gratitude can play a significant role in pain management. Living with a grateful heart has given me a sense of control over pain, knowing that a gratitude mindset and subsequent emotional well-being can influence my physical health.

Gratitude & Cardiovascular Health: A Vital Connection

Integrating gratitude into daily life has profound implications for cardiovascular health and overall well-being. Scientific evidence and biblical teachings converge to affirm the therapeutic value of cultivating a grateful heart and a grateful mindset. By embracing gratitude as an initiative-taking health strategy, individuals can empower themselves to mitigate the adverse effects of negative emotions, promote cardiovascular resilience, and foster a healthier, more fulfilling life.

The Bible also emphasizes the profound impact of gratitude on physical health. Proverbs 17:22 states, "A cheerful heart is good medicine, but a crushed spirit dries up the bones." This biblical wisdom underscores the therapeutic value of maintaining a joyful and thankful heart, highlighting its ability to promote healing and resilience in the face of physical challenges.

As humans, we typically have negative biases about life situations. This means our first thought about a communication or situation is, "What's wrong with this?" The problem is that when negativity becomes extreme, manifesting itself in emotions such as stress, anxiety, and anger, it can trigger a cascade of physiological reactions within the body, contributing to increased blood pressure. This link between emotional states and physical health has been extensively studied. These studies increasingly show that gratitude practices can significantly impact cardiovascular health. One notable study in 1995 highlighted those individuals who regularly experienced and expressed gratitude showed improved heart rate variability—a critical marker of heart health—compared to those who did not engage in such practices (Smith & Jones, 1995). This finding suggests that cultivating a grateful mindset can directly influence physiological processes related to cardiovascular function, potentially lowering the risk of hypertension and related complications.

From a medical perspective, recent studies have explored how gratitude influences physiological mechanisms linked to blood pressure regulation. Gratitude practices have been shown to activate the parasympathetic nervous system, promoting relaxation responses that counteract the physiological stress responses associated with hypertension. This activation helps reduce heart rate and systemic vascular resistance, lowering overall blood pressure levels. For instance, a longitudinal study over five years observed that individuals who supported a regular gratitude journal experienced significant reductions in systolic and diastolic blood pressure compared to a control group (Davis et al., 2021). These findings suggest that consistent engagement with gratitude can contribute to long-term improvements in cardiovascular health by modulating blood pressure dynamics.

Gratitude & Focus: Rewiring the ADHD Brain

Certainly, while ADHD isn't directly addressed in the Bible, there are passages that offer comfort, encouragement, and guidance for managing traits associated with it—like impulsivity, inattention, restlessness, and difficulty staying focused. "But he said to me, 'My grace is sufficient for you, for my power is made perfect in weakness.' Therefore, I will boast all the more gladly of my weaknesses, so that the power of Christ may rest upon me." (2 Corinthians 12:9)

This verse is a reminder that even when we feel limited by our challenges, God's grace is sufficient. Practicing gratitude for God's strength in our weaknesses can shift our focus from frustration to a deep sense of dependence on Him, helping us find peace and focus in His strength. Where the mind often feels at odds with itself, and impulsive actions constantly thwart intentions gratitude can be a powerful coping and healing tool amidst this struggle. By focusing on gratitude, individuals can shift their perspective from frustration to appreciation, finding moments of peace and clarity even amid chaos.

Attention Deficit Hyperactivity Disorder (ADHD) is a neurodevelopmental disorder characterized by persistent patterns of inattention, impulsiveness, and hyperactivity that can significantly impair daily functioning. While ADHD is commonly associated with children, it also affects adults, albeit often undiagnosed or misdiagnosed. Managing ADHD involves a multifaceted approach, including medication, therapy, and behavioral interventions.

> *"I've said for many years that I have ADHD, and I'm proud of it." ~Elon Musk*[5]

Emerging research suggests that incorporating a grateful mindset into treatment strategies can offer profound benefits in restoring focus and improving overall well-being for individuals with ADHD. This chapter explores the intersection between gratitude and ADHD, examining how cultivating gratitude can positively affect attention regulation, emotional resilience, and interpersonal relationships in children and adults.

Before we get to clinical, and remember I am no psychiatrist, and delve into the role of gratitude in managing ADHD, it is crucial to understand the challenges posed by this disorder. ADHD manifests differently in everyone, with symptoms ranging from difficulty sustaining attention, organizing tasks, and following through instructions, to impulsivity and excessive fidgeting or talking. These symptoms can interfere with academic performance, work productivity, and social interactions, leading to frustration, low self-esteem, and impaired quality of life.

Children with ADHD often struggle academically, experiencing challenges in concentrating on schoolwork, completing assignments, and staying organized. As a result, they may face academic underachievement and negative feedback from teachers and peers, furthering feelings of inadequacy and frustration. Similarly, adults with ADHD may meet difficulties in maintaining employment, managing finances, and sustaining relationships due to impulsivity, forgetfulness, and disorganization.

The Power of Presence: Introducing Gratitude as Therapy

Before retiring in 2011, I taught Sunday School to many beautiful 6th graders on the traditional architecture of the Greek Orthodox Church. Among these bright young minds, I encountered a remarkable young girl named Sophia. Over the years, I formed a close friendship with her family, particularly her Yaya. Her mother, a young widow, navigating the complexities of raising a child with unique challenges, relied heavily on Yaya Mary. Sophia's diagnosis of ADHD stood as a towering obstacle in a world that often expects conformity above all else.

Sophia had always been a whirlwind of energy and ideas as a child. Her Yaya and mother loved her for it, but she also knew the challenges it brought. Sophia was diagnosed with ADHD when she was seven. The constant motion and the never-ending stream of thought made it difficult for Sophia to focus on school and often led to disruptions at home. For Sophia, her ADHD meant homework assignments left unfinished, impulsive reactions during conversations and an overwhelming sensation of being misunderstood by peers and teachers alike.

Early on, her mother, determined to help her daughter, sought various therapies and interventions. During one of the sessions, Sophia's therapist introduced the concept of incorporating gratitude into daily life as a therapeutic exercise. The therapist explained that appreciation isn't just about saying thank you but a transformative practice that could help Sophia slow down, reflect, and control her impulsive thoughts and actions.

The therapist emphasized that gratitude could function as a grounding mechanism, anchoring Sophia in moments of mindfulness. This approach resonated deeply with Sophia's mother, who was already familiar with gratitude from her spiritual practices. Together, they embarked on a journey to weave gratitude into the fabric of their daily lives.

They started with small steps: keeping a gratitude journal, expressing thanks before meals, and reflecting on positive moments at the end of each day.

This practice of gratitude began to show promising results. As young as she was, the brilliant Sophia found that she could better manage her emotions and reactions by focusing on what she was thankful for, the moments of stillness and reflection allowed her to develop a greater sense of self-awareness, which helped her navigate the challenges of ADHD. It wasn't an overnight transformation, but with persistence and support, Sophia started to see improvements in her ability to concentrate and engage more calmly with her environment.

As we have seen, gratitude as a therapeutic tool extends beyond ADHD. In numerous studies, gratitude has been shown to profoundly impact mental health and well-being. It can reduce symptoms of depression and anxiety, improve sleep quality, and enhance overall life satisfaction. For individuals with ADHD, who often struggle with emotional regulation and impulsivity, gratitude offers a valuable tool for fostering a more balanced and mindful approach to life.

Developing a grateful mindset and incorporating gratitude into daily routines can benefit children like Sophia. It provides them with a structured way to recognize and appreciate the positive aspects of their lives, which can be grounding and stabilizing.

This practice can also strengthen the parent-child relationship as they share moments of gratitude and reflection.

In the context of our Sunday School lessons, the architecture of the (Greek) Orthodox Church also offered a unique opportunity to explore themes of gratitude and reflection. The church's intricate designs and sacred spaces are imbued with reverence and thankfulness by instructing the children about these elements. At the time, without knowing it, I was instilling in them an appreciation for the beauty and significance of their spiritual heritage.

The traditional architecture of the Greek Orthodox Church, with its domes, iconography, and symbolism, is a physical manifestation of the principles of faith and gratitude. The grandeur of the domes, reaching towards the heavens, symbolizes the aspirations of the human spirit to connect with the divine. The icons, rich with imagery and meaning, remind the faithful of the saints and martyrs who exemplified lives of gratitude and devotion. Each element of the church's architecture tells a story of faith, perseverance, and thankfulness.

As I taught these lessons to the 6th graders, I often reflected on how the principles of gratitude could be woven into their own lives. Just as the church's architecture is a testament to centuries of faith and devotion, our daily gratitude practices can build a solid foundation for personal growth and well-being. By nurturing a sense of thankfulness, we can cultivate a resilient spirit capable of weathering life's challenges.

In the years following my retirement, I have seen some former students, including Sophia, grow into remarkable individuals. Their journeys are a testament to the power of gratitude and the enduring lessons learned within the walls of our Sunday School. Sophia has embraced gratitude as a cornerstone of her life. Her mother's unwavering support and the therapeutic exercises they practiced together have helped her navigate the complexities of ADHD with grace and resilience.

Sophia's story powerfully reminds us that gratitude is not just a fleeting emotion but a deliberate practice that can transform lives. This lesson extends beyond the individual, influencing families, communities, and society. In a world that often values speed and efficiency over mindfulness and reflection, gratitude offers a counterbalance, encouraging us to slow down, appreciate the present moment, and acknowledge the blessings surrounding us.

The New Role of Gratitude in ADHD Management

Gratitude, the appreciation of what is valuable and meaningful in one's life, has garnered increasing attention in positive psychology for its profound effects on mental health and well-being. Research suggests that cultivating gratitude can enhance resilience, foster positive emotions, and improve overall life satisfaction. Moreover, gratitude practices have been associated with reduced symptoms of depression, anxiety, and stress, indicating its potential therapeutic value for individuals with ADHD.

In ADHD management, adopting a grateful mindset can offer several benefits that complement traditional treatment approaches. By shifting focus from deficits to strengths, gratitude encourages individuals to recognize and appreciate their accomplishments, no matter how small, thereby enhancing self-esteem and self-efficacy. For children with ADHD, this can be particularly empowering, as it instills a sense of competence and agency in managing their symptoms.

Furthermore, gratitude promotes mindfulness and present-moment awareness, which are essential for individuals with ADHD who often struggle with distractibility and impulsivity. By grounding attention in the here and now, developing the habits discussed later, such as keeping a gratitude journal, in any of the forms, or engaging in mindful gratitude exercises, can help individuals with ADHD regulate attention and resist impulsive behaviors.

Moreover, gratitude fosters positive social connections and prosocial behavior, which is crucial for individuals with ADHD in building supportive relationships and navigating social challenges. By expressing gratitude towards others and acknowledging their contributions, individuals with ADHD can strengthen interpersonal bonds and cultivate a sense of belonging within their communities.

Relationships

---

*"Let us be grateful to the people who make us happy; they are the charming gardeners who make our souls blossom."~ **Baxter Black**[6]*

IMAGE THE POWER OF A single word to transform your relationships, nurture and strengthen the bonds you hold dear, and forge new connections that can change your life. In this chapter, we uncover the profound impact of gratitude on our interactions with others. We delve into the simple yet profound act of expressing thanks and how it can breathe new life into your relationships. But this wisdom isn't just modern insight but deeply rooted in ancient teachings. Read on as we explore how the Bible illuminates the transformative power of gratitude, revealing its timeless role in fostering healthy, enduring relationships.

Baxter Black (January 10, 1945 – June 10, 2022) was a renowned American cowboy poet, veterinarian, and commentator who captivated audiences with his humor and reflections on rural life. Born at the Brooklyn Naval Hospital in New York, he was raised in Las Cruces, New Mexico where he pursued veterinary medicine at New Mexico State University and Colorado State University, earning his Doctor of Veterinary Medicine degree. He specialized in large animal care, particularly cattle, which provided him with firsthand experiences that later enriched his storytelling.

Transitioning from veterinary practice in the early 1980s, Black became a prominent cowboy poet and storyteller. Which is where I first met him briefly, at the National Cowboy Poetry Gathering, a cowboy poet event in Elko, Nevada, in the late 80s. I was at the event with my best compadre at the time "Ranger" Dave Wesley; a crazy Montana cowboy and barbed wire real estate executive, who loved cowboy poetry. Black's works, characterized by wit and authenticity, resonated with both rural and urban audiences. He authored over 30 poetry and fiction books, selling more than two million copies.

His quote, "Let us be grateful to the people who make us happy; they are the charming gardeners who make our souls blossom," reflects the heart of his poetic and storytelling philosophy. Through his writings and performances, Black often emphasized the importance of recognizing the ordinary yet profound relationships that shape our lives. For him, gratitude wasn't an abstract virtue, it was a tangible practice rooted in everyday encounters and the connections forged within rural and ranching communities.

Black's writing also suggests that gratitude is a form of stewardship. By appreciating and nurturing the relationships that bring us a sense of contentment, we contribute to their growth and ensure that the seeds of happiness continue to bear fruit for others. This perspective aligns with his larger belief in the interconnectedness of rural life, where stewardship extends beyond land and livestock to include relationships and community bonds. Black's quote invites us to cherish the people who bring beauty and vitality to our lives, acknowledging their role in helping us flourish.

In the 1980s, during my travels to New Mexico while inspecting real estate properties for my firm, one thing was certain: if Baxter Black was performing, Ranger Dave made sure we were there. At the time, I wasn't a believer, but there was something about Black's performances and public statements that left a lasting impression. Even though he may not have overtly identified as a religious figure, it was clear that he held a deep respect for faith and spirituality. His words were infused with a reverence for life, a humility, and a sense of gratitude—qualities I would come to recognize much later in my life as core Christian values. As I reflect on those moments, I now see how his messages were shaping me, long before I fully understood their depth.

Nurturing and Strengthening Existing Relationships

The Bible offers valuable insights into various aspects of human life, including relationships. Here, we will explore what the Bible says about gratitude in the context of nurturing and strengthening existing relationships and forging new ones, uncovering the timeless teachings and experiences that cultivate gratitude in my interactions with others.

A troubling increase in divorces and breakups marks the current landscape of relationships. In popular media, we often hear partners citing a lack of attention or appreciation as reasons for leaving or engaging in infidelity. This underscores the hazardous nature of taking our loved ones for granted.

Gratitude plays a pivotal role in nurturing and strengthening existing relationships. The Bible guides us in expressing gratitude to deepen our connections with loved ones. 1 Corinthians 13:4-7: "Love is patient and kind; love does not envy or boast; it is not arrogant or rude. It does not insist on its own way; it is not irritable or resentful; it does not rejoice at wrongdoing but rejoices with the truth. Love bears all things, believes all things, hopes all things, endures all things." These verses from Corinthians remind us of the qualities of love, which are closely intertwined with gratitude. Gratitude demonstrates kindness and humility, fostering trust and hope within relationships. By expressing gratitude, we embody the essence of love and strengthen our connections with others.

To address the challenges in modern relationships, it is crucial to cultivate an increased awareness of gratitude. Substantial evidence, both in science and in the root of science (the Bible), supports the notion that expressing gratitude to loved ones through acts of kindness, affirmation, and thoughtful gestures can profoundly nurture these relationships.

Ecclesiastes 4:9-10: "Two are better than one, because they have a good reward for their toil. For if they fall, one will lift up his fellow. But woe to him who is alone when he falls and has not another to lift him up!" This passage highlights the value of companionship and the support of having someone by our side. Gratitude allows us to acknowledge the blessings of having loved ones who stand with us in times of need. It strengthens our bonds by recognizing mutual assistance and interdependence within relationships.

One key takeaway from research on relationships is that regular gratitude can significantly strengthen them. When we consciously appreciate our loved ones, we reaffirm the value they bring to our lives.

In relationships, while saying "thank you" is undoubtedly important, it should not be the extent of our gratitude expression. Loved ones may come to expect this as the norm, so it is essential to go beyond the basics.

The secret to effectively expressing gratitude through spoken words lies in the nuances. This includes incorporating observations, emphasizing our dependence on the person, and conveying our feelings for them. By doing so, we strengthen our emotional connection with the individual.

Observation is a fundamental aspect of expressing gratitude in relationships. Often, our loved ones perform acts of kindness or demonstrate their affection in ways that go unnoticed. It is incumbent upon us to recognize and appreciate these gestures.

Throughout the Bible, gratitude emerges as a unifying thread that runs through relationship teachings and principles. Whether nurturing existing bonds or forging new connections, gratitude is a foundational element that enriches our interactions with others. Colossians 3:15 (NIV) - "Let the peace of Christ rule in your hearts, since as members of one body you were called to peace. And be thankful." Gratitude is not merely a fleeting sentiment but a disposition of the heart. It is a call to be thankful in all aspects of our lives, including our relationships. When we carry a heart of gratitude, we invite peace and harmony into our interactions with others, both old and new.

Expressing gratitude goes beyond acknowledging acts of kindness. Remember my experience with my friend David and his wife after dinner at my house? David's simple act of asking for help with the washing of the dishes can have a profound impact on friendships. When acknowledged and appreciated, this act of gratitude can make a significant difference in the dynamics of any relationship. Expressing gratitude for these small yet meaningful actions validate their significance, and conveying their impact is essential to David's and his wife's relationship and their relationship with my wife and me.

Expressing gratitude goes beyond mere acknowledgment; it also involves conveying how these acts of kindness made us feel. Sharing our emotions and sentiments regarding these gestures deepens our connection with our loved ones. For example, if someone opened a door for us, we could tell them how it made us feel special or appreciated.

Acknowledging our dependence on others can be challenging, yet it is vital to expressing gratitude. Recognizing that we need people in our lives is essential for fostering more robust relationships. It is also important to communicate this dependency. People influence our lives, and we must communicate why we need them effectively. We enhance our relationships by articulating the significance of their presence and support. This openness fosters under-standing, empathy, and a deeper connection.

Gratitude should not be confined solely to what others do for us. It should encompass their presence and the intangible ways they enrich our lives. By looking beyond actions, we discover numerous op-portunities for gratitude.

Gratitude in Forging New Relationships

Gratitude nurtures existing relationships and plays a pivotal role in forging new connections. Its transformative power extends beyond maintaining bonds to attract and build relationships with new individuals. Gratitude has the remarkable ability to make individuals more positive. A sense of thankful-ness leads to feeling cared for, appreciated, and loved. This positiveness, in turn, influences how we interact with others.

When we cultivate a grateful mindset, we radiate positivity. Happy individuals are inherently more pleasant to be around. This positivity not only influ-ences our interactions but also makes us more lik-able. This is where the Law of Attraction comes into play. The Law of Attraction states that like attracts like. Therefore, we attract other positive individuals when we emit positive energy through gratitude. This constructive interaction creates fertile ground for new relationships to blossom.

A fundamental principle of gratitude is that kindness begets kindness. When we express appreciation and treat others kindly, they are more inclined to reciprocate. Optimistic people tend to attract positive individuals, fostering an environment conducive to building new relationships. Gratitude allows individuals to recognize acts of kindness. When we feel thankful, we are more attuned to the support and assistance we receive from others. This heightened awareness of kindness motivates us to reciprocate.

Proverbs 18:24 states, " A man of many companions may come to ruin, but there is a friend who sticks closer than a brother." This verse highlights the value of genuine friendships and the impact of the people we surround ourselves with. Gratitude can serve as a magnet, attracting kindred spirits who appreciate and reciprocate acts of goodwill. Being a grateful individual makes us more likely to attract positive and supportive friends.

Gratitude has been shown to induce pro-social behavior, making individuals more inclined to help others and offer emotional support. This inclination is rooted in the perception of kindness and the desire to reciprocate acts of goodwill. Gratitude is linked to increased energy, and happiness is strongly associated with pro-social behavior. When energized and content, we are more willing to approach others, help them overcome challenges, and provide emotional support.

Individuals who adopt a grateful mindset and actively practice gratitude are more approachable and helpful. As a result, they attract a broader cross-section of people into their social networks. Gratitude is a magnet, drawing individuals who appreciate and resonate with positive outlooks on life.

I have grandchildren who have recently entered college. College students frequently rely on the support of their families and, in some ways, their friends. This support can come in various forms, such as financial assistance, emotional encouragement, or practical help like rides or meals. When they express gratitude for this support, it strengthens their relationships and encourages continued aid. People are more likely to help those who appreciate their efforts.

Additionally, gratitude fosters community and mutual support among the students. When my college-bound grandchildren express thanks for the help they receive, it not only benefits them but also creates a positive atmosphere that encourages others to be supportive. This interchange has led to a network of family members and individuals willing to help my grandchildren and each other, reducing emotional stress.

In addition, gratitude can lead to new opportunities. For example, my grandson, Mace, is a first-year Air Force Academy student. His genuine appreciation for the guidance and mentorship of several professors, military instructors, and, most certainly, his appointed advisor has opened doors for future academic and military career opportunities.

Professors and advisors are likelier to invest their time and resources in students who show gratitude, creating a beneficial cycle of support and growth.

Gratitude also helps Mace manage stress and maintain a positive outlook during challenging times. His first year at the Academy will be demanding, with military and academic pressures, social challenges, and financial constraints. When Mace focuses on what he is grateful for, he subtly shifts his perspective from scarcity to abundance, recognizing the resources and support he has rather than dwelling on what he lacks.

We have learned that a grateful mindset can also lead to financial benefits through better mental health and decision-making. Studies have shown that individuals who regularly practice gratitude experience lower stress and anxiety levels, leading to better financial decision-making. For college students, this means being more mindful of their spending, prioritizing their needs, and avoiding impulsive purchases that can lead to financial strain.

Furthermore, gratitude can enhance networking skills. Expressing appreciation for the opportunities and connections they encounter leaves a positive impression on others, which can lead to more meaningful and beneficial relationships with peers, professors, and potential employers. Networking is a critical aspect of career development, and gratitude can give Mace an edge in building a robust professional network.

Gratitude, Relationships, and Economic Benefits: A Holistic View

Gratitude and the Law of Attraction work together to develop new relationships by creating a positive aura around individuals. This positivity attracts like-minded people, fostering an environment where new relationships can thrive. By expressing gratitude, individuals like Mace strengthen existing bonds and pave the way for new connections that offer support and opportunities.

Mace's realization of the economic benefits of gratitude highlights how this positive mindset can lead to tangible benefits. Expressing gratitude for the support he receives encourages continued assistance and creates a network of mutual support among his peers. This network can provide practical help, emotional support, and potential career opportunities, all contributing to Mace's overall well-being and success.

Gratitude also plays a crucial role in maintaining a positive outlook during challenging times. For college students, who often face significant stress and financial constraints, focusing on gratitude can shift their perspective and help them manage these challenges more effectively. By recognizing and appreciating the support they receive, students can build resilience and maintain their motivation to succeed.

Gratitude is a powerful tool that can transform relationships and create economic benefits. By cultivating a grateful mindset, individuals can attract positive energy, build meaningful connections, and enhance their well-being. For Mace and other college students, this means surviving and thriving in their academic and personal lives.

The Interplay of Gratitude and the Law of Attraction

The Law of Attraction suggests that our thoughts and emotions can influence our reality. When we focus on positive thoughts and feelings, such as gratitude, we attract positive experiences and people into our lives. This principle can be seen in how gratitude fosters new relationships and enhances existing ones.

By developing out our gratitude mindset, we align our energy with positivity and abundance. This alignment attracts others who share similar energies, creating a harmonious environment where relationships can flourish. For example, when Mace expresses gratitude for the support he receives, he attracts individuals who are willing to offer further assistance and encouragement. This positive cycle reinforces the benefits of appreciation and strengthens his social network.

The Law of Attraction also highlights the importance of visualization and intention-setting. When we visualize our goals and express gratitude for what we have, we create a powerful combination that can manifest our desires. For Mace, this means visualizing academic and career success while expressing gratitude for the support he currently receives. This practice can attract opportunities that align with his goals and aspirations.

Gratitude's Role in Building Community

Gratitude is not just a personal practice but a communal one. When individuals express gratitude, it creates a ripple effect that can influence entire communities. In college, gratitude can foster a sense of belonging and mutual support among students.

Mace's gratitude for the help he receives from friends and family can inspire others to adopt a similar mindset. As more students express appreciation for the support they receive, a culture of gratitude that benefits everyone is created. This culture encourages students to help one another, share resources, and offer emotional support, creating a stronger and more resilient community.

Gratitude can also enhance the relationship between students and faculty. Students like Mace express authentic appreciation for their professors' guidance and support, fostering a positive and collaborative learning environment. Professors are likely to go above and beyond for students who show gratitude, leading to better academic outcomes and increased mentorship and professional development opportunities.

Benefits of Gratitude for College Students

For college students like Mace, whose entire college experience is paid for by the United States Air Force, the economic benefits of gratitude extend beyond immediate financial assistance. Gratitude can lead to better financial habits, improved mental health, and enhanced military career prospects.

Practicing gratitude can help students manage their finances more effectively. Students can develop a mindset of abundance that encourages mindful spending and saving by focusing on what they have rather than what they lack. This can lead to better financial decision-making and reduced financial stress.

Gratitude can also improve mental health, linked to financial well-being. Students with a grateful mindset experience lower stress and anxiety levels, leading to improved academic performance and overall health. This, in turn, can reduce healthcare costs and improve students' ability to focus on their studies and career goals.

Furthermore, gratitude can enhance career prospects by improving networking skills and fostering positive relationships with potential employers. When students express gratitude for internships, job opportunities, and professional connections, it leaves a positive impression that can lead to further opportunities. Employers are more likely to hire and promote individuals who demonstrate appreciation and a positive attitude.

The Grateful Leader

> *"Being grateful for the experience of opportunities placed in our path, both rich and barren, separates privilege from entitlement"* –*the Author.*

DISCOVER HOW A GRATEFUL MINDSET can enhance leadership skills, inspire teams, and lead to more impactful decision-making at work.

Imagine unlocking a secret power that enhances physical and mental well-being, transforms relationships, supercharges your career, and turns your workplace into a hub of positivity and productivity. This chapter dives into the surprising, game-changing role that gratitude can play in your professional life. From making managers more effective and boosting decision-making abilities to increasing productivity and opening doors to new mentorship opportunities, gratitude is the key to achieving your career goals and creating a more enjoyable work environment. Get ready to discover how a simple act of gratitude can revolutionize your path to success.

In the early 1980s, leaving a successful commercial real estate banking career, I traveled to and worked in Albuquerque, New Mexico, as the General Partner of a real estate investment and development partnership. In those days, 40-something years ago, I was scouting land to build what was then called new-era urban residential apartments.

I met and became fast friends with two remarkably talented commercial real estate landmen. First, Dave "Ranger Dave" Wesley, a fearless Montana cowboy and Viet Nam combat veteran turned New Mexico real estate specialist and restaurant entrepreneur (505 Restaurant, Albuquerque, NM). Secondly, New Mexico's #1 commercial land broker, Elmo Rhoton, a former PRCA Bronk rider from Amarillo, Texas. My friendship with these men and their families extended through the next four decades, though Elmo passed away in 2008. No other men taught me more about respect and appreciation for "barbed wire real estate" and the cowboy way of life as these men did. As my relationship with these men grew, I fell deeply in love with the Western heritage and breathtaking landscapes that define New Mexico and the vast expanse of West Texas. The sweeping deserts, towering mesas, and rugged mountains became more than just scenery to me; they represented a way of life that I had long admired from a distance. This infatuation was not merely with the land but with the essence of Southwest culture, history, and people.

These two men were, in my mind, the embodiment of the Western spirit. Elmo, with his quiet cowboy wisdom and steadfast dedication to his family, work, and stewardship of the land, and Ranger Dave, with his unyielding resilience and determination to make a positive economic impact for the people of New Mexico, were instrumental in guiding my numerous land investments in New Mexico.

However, as time went on, I made a significant mistake. Instead of simply learning from my time with these men and being grateful for the experiences they provided, I began to adopt their characteristics as my brand. I saw their attributes as qualities to admire and aspects of my identity. The shift was subtle initially, but the idolatry grew more pronounced as I became more engrossed in my work and the surrounding lifestyle.

The allure of embodying the Western archetype was strong. Something was intoxicating about being seen as a Texan who exemplified grit, perseverance, a hard-driven deal maker, and authentically Western. I began to lose sight of the fact that these characteristics, though present in my life, were not inherently mine but qualities I had the privilege of witnessing and learning from.

This conflation was not just a personal failure; it influenced my work at the time. At forty-five years old, I wanted to be seen (branded) as someone who had completely mastered the challenges of developing barbed wire real estate. Though successful, I was still a student, learning and growing from my experiences.

It took time and reflection to realize that my true strength lay not in adopting their identities but in appreciating the unique journey I was on. The experiences and lessons I gleaned from Elmo, Ranger Dave, and the many others along the way were gifts. They provided me with insights and perspectives that enriched my life and work. I am deeply grateful.

This realization was a turning point. Years later, as I began writing, it allowed me to reframe my narrative and writing. Instead of presenting myself as an embodiment of the Western ideal, I began to focus on my gratitude for my experiences and the authenticity of my journey. This shift would bring my work to a new level of depth and honesty.

Looking back, I see how essential it was to make this distinction. I am grateful for their impact on my work and still acknowledge my path and the personal growth that came with it.

Cowboy's Communication Mastery

Looking back, my observation of Elmo Rhoton centered on how his masterful communication style and gratitude mindset helped him create an independent commercial real estate business that developed into one of the most successful in New Mexico.

Elmo had spent the earlier part of his life in the dusty rodeo arenas of the PRCA circuit, earning his reputation as one of the finest bronc riders in the business. With countless buckles and scars to his name, he'd ridden the wildest horses and stared danger in the eye for years. However, as the years passed and his family and body began to show the wear and tear of his rodeo career, Elmo knew it was time for a change.

Retirement was a challenging decision for Elmo. The adrenaline rush of the rodeo, the cheers of the crowd, and the camaraderie of fellow riders were hard to leave behind. But he also knew that his family and his body could not take the punishment forever, and he wanted a future that didn't involve constant pain and injuries and being away from his wife and two daughters. That is when he stumbled upon a new passion—real estate.

Elmo was always a people person. He had a gift for connecting with others, a skill he had honed during his years on the rodeo circuit. Elmo knew that to succeed in real estate, he would have to use that gift to build relationships with buyers and landowners looking to buy or sell their ranches and barbed wire real estate. And that is where the power of gratitude came into play.

So, I can see Elmo starting his journey by practicing daily gratitude.

When he represented me in my acquisitions in New Mexico, I could be with him daily for weeks. Though not necessarily in a structured way, Elmo's day was usually fluid. Every morning, before he began his work, Elmo would sit down and reflect on what he was grateful for. He would think about the love of his family, the friends he'd made in the rodeo, and the opportunities that lay ahead in his real estate career. It was not always easy, especially on days when Elmo felt the aches and pains of his past injuries. My friend had grit, and he persisted.

With his newfound mindset of gratitude, Elmo set out to build relationships with buyers and landowners. He realized that connecting with people went beyond just selling a piece of land – it was about understanding their dreams, aspirations, and concerns. He listened to their stories, learned about their families, and genuinely cared about their well-being. The gratitude and affinity continued to develop for his new lifestyle and the community he set out to serve.

One of his first clients was the Monroe family, a couple in their fifties looking to sell their ranch and down-size. They had lived on the land for decades, raising their children and building a life together. The decision to sell was not easy for them, and they were apprehensive about letting go of the place they had called home for so long.

Elmo approached the Monroe family with empathy and a grateful heart. He listened to their memories, hopes for the future, and emotional attachment to their ranch. He made them feel heard and understood, and they began trusting him.

As they navigated selling their ranch, Elmo continued to practice gratitude in every interaction. He thanked the Monroes for choosing him as their realtor, for sharing their stories, and for the opportunity to help them through this transition. His sincerity and appreciation for their trust shone through in every conversation, making the Monroes feel valued and cared for.

The Monroe ranch soon found a new owner, and the couple moved to a smaller property better suited to their needs. Elmo stayed in touch with them, inviting them to local events and dinners and helping them adjust to their new neighborhood. The Monroes, in turn, referred him to friends and family looking to buy or sell land.

Word of Elmo's unique approach began to spread, and his real estate career blossomed. He helped ranchers find the perfect properties and made it a point to express gratitude to every client, big or small. His positive mindset and genuine appreciation for his clients set him apart in the industry.

One of his most challenging transactions was with the Donovan family, a group of siblings who had inherited a vast ranch but couldn't agree on what to do with it. Their conflicting opinions and long-standing family tensions made the process complicated and emotional.

Elmo knew that he needed to foster a sense of gratitude within the Donovan family. He encouraged them to appreciate the land they had inherited, the memories it held, and the opportunities it presented. He organized a family gathering on the ranch, allowing them to reconnect with each other and the land.

During the gathering, Elmo shared stories of his rodeo days, emphasizing the importance of teamwork, and supporting one another. He expressed gratitude for the relationships he had built in his career, especially the Donovan family, for allowing him to join their journey.

Slowly but surely, the Donovan's began to see the potential of their ranch and the importance of their family bond. They eventually agreed on a plan that satisfied everyone's needs, and the property was sold to a buyer who shared their vision.

As the years passed, Elmo remembered his rodeo days with fondness, grateful for the lessons he had learned and the people he had met along the way. He knew that gratitude had transformed his life, allowing him to ride the broncs of the barbed wire real estate corals with the same passion and dedication he had brought to the rodeo arena. And in the end, the power of gratitude made him not just a successful real estate salesperson but a truly fulfilled and content individual.

Studies have shown that gratitude can give you the energy boost you need to focus on your career goals. In the research, participants were asked to write down their goals. Those who were more grateful reported more remarkable progress towards meeting the goals that they had set for themselves by the end of their studies.

Being thankful naturally boosts your motivation and energy levels. It can change how your brain functions. You will also be able to enjoy a better quality of sleep. All these things work together to help energize you and give you the boost you need to focus on your aims.

Gratitude Fuels Creativity in Work

With health issues bearing down on me later in life, embarking on heavy writing goals might seem impossible. The gratitude I felt for being given the gift of writing and the unwavering love of the Lord gave me the strength to persevere and the energy to accomplish what seemed impossible.

My journey into non-fiction writing at such a stage in life was unexpected. Diagnosed with degenerative arthritis and metastatic prostate cancer meant every day became a battle against pain and fatigue. There were moments when negative thoughts threatened to consume me, when the weight of my physical limitations seemed too heavy to bear. However, amidst the darkness, a glimmer of light emerged – the feeling of gratitude.

I began researching and authoring this book, and as I did, gratitude became my lifeline, my beacon of hope amid adversity. Instead of dwelling on what I had lost or could not do, I focused on the blessings surrounding me. From the warmth of the morning sun streaming through my window to the gentle touch of Mary's hand, each moment became a reason to give thanks. Gratitude shifted my perspective from my natural negative bias to appreciation, allowing me to find joy even amid pain.

Central to my journey as a new believer was the unwavering love of the Lord. Through prayer and reflection, I found solace in knowing I was never alone in my struggles. The faith that sustained me through these times gave me the courage to face each day with renewed determination. Through this faith, I found the strength to navigate the challenges ahead, knowing God's love would guide me.

Moreover, I was blessed with the support of many God-fearing individuals who walked alongside me on this journey. Whether it was the kind words of a friend or the compassionate care of my faith community, their presence was a constant reminder of God's grace. Their acts of kindness and encouragement fueled my spirit, motivating me to press on despite the obstacles in my path.

As I delved deeper into the world of writing, I discovered that gratitude was not just a source of comfort but also a wellspring of energy. It was gratitude that fueled my creativity, igniting a passion within me to share my experiences with the world. Instead of allowing my health issues to define me, I embraced them as part of my narrative, weaving them into the fabric of my writing with honesty and authenticity.

With each word I penned, I found a sense of purpose that transcended my physical limitations. Writing became my sanctuary, where I could pour out my heart and soul without reservation. Through writing, I found healing for myself and others who resonated with my words and found solace in knowing they were not alone in their struggles.

Gratitude became the driving force behind my writing and the goal of finishing this book, propelling me forward even when the journey seemed daunting. Instead of focusing on the obstacles that stood in my way, I focused on the blessings surrounding me. Each day became an opportunity to express gratitude for the gift of life and the chance to pursue my passion.

Moreover, writing became an expression of gratitude—a way to thank God for the experiences that had shaped me and the lessons I had learned along the way. Through my writing, I sought to inspire others to embrace gratitude as a way of life, knowing firsthand its transformative power.

My journey into writing continued through eight was not just about accomplishing goals but about embracing life with a grateful heart and steadfast faith. As I look back on the path I have traveled, I realize it was through the practice of gratitude that I found the energy to accomplish my very arduous writing goals and, in doing so, discovered a sense of purpose and fulfillment that transcended my wildest dreams.

In leadership, one often encounters a myriad of strategies, philosophies, and techniques. From charismatic authority to strategic planning, the approaches are diverse. However, amidst this diversity, one often overlooked but profoundly impactful mindset is gratitude. Being deeply embedded in religious, philosophical, and organizational traditions is critical to unlocking leadership potential. Drawing from diverse sources, including biblical narratives, modern organizational settings, and timeless wisdom, we explore how embracing a gratitude mindset can transform leadership abilities.

Joseph's biblical narrative is a compelling example of how gratitude can shape leadership. Joseph, sold into slavery by his brothers, endured numerous trials, including false accusations and imprisonment. Despite these hardships, Joseph never lost his gratitude towards God. In Genesis 41:16, when Pharaoh sought interpretation for his dreams, Joseph attributed his ability to God, saying, "I cannot do it, but God will give Pharaoh the answer he desires." This humility and acknowledgment of divine assistance exemplify Joseph's gratitude.

Joseph's attitude of gratitude extended beyond personal circumstances to his leadership in Egypt. When his brothers, who had once betrayed him, sought help during a famine, Joseph forgave them and provided for them generously. In Genesis 50:20, Joseph declares, "You intended to harm me, but God intended it for good to accomplish what is now being done, the saving of many lives." His gratitude towards God's providence enabled him to lead with compassion, forgiveness, and a broader perspective.

The Power of Gratitude in Modern Leadership

In the context of modern organizational leadership, the story of the Trump Organization provides a lens through which to examine the role of gratitude.

While controversies and critiques surround the organization and the current consequential President of the United States, one aspect often highlighted is Donald Trump's gratitude towards his employees, his staff, and his current cabinet members. Numerous accounts from former employees attest to Trump's habit of sending handwritten notes of appreciation and recognition for their hard work and dedication.

Despite varying opinions on Trump's leadership style, his emphasis on acknowledging and appreciating his team members demonstrates the power of gratitude in fostering loyalty and motivation. By recognizing his employees' contributions, Trump cultivated a culture where individuals felt valued and empowered, enhancing productivity and organizational effectiveness.

In the world of professional rodeo, the Professional Rodeo Cowboys Association (PRCA) stands as a testament to the importance of gratitude in leadership. The PRCA, an organization dedicated to promoting the sport of rodeo, thrives on the appreciation of its participants and supporters. Rodeo athletes, often facing physical challenges and financial uncertainties, express gratitude towards sponsors, fans, and fellow competitors for their support.

The PRCA leadership understands the significance of fostering a culture of gratitude. By acknowledging the sacrifices and contributions of rodeo participants and supporters, the organization cultivates a sense of belonging and unity within the community. This culture of gratitude enhances the rodeo experience and strengthens its members' resilience and camaraderie.

The stories drawn from biblical narratives, modern organizational settings, and specific examples such as the Trump Organization and the PRCA highlight the profound impact of gratitude on leadership ability. Just as Joseph's journey of appreciation transformed his leadership in ancient Egypt, he exemplified the spiritual and personal growth catalyzed by appreciation.

As individuals and leaders, embracing a mindset of gratitude unlocks hidden potential, fosters personal growth, and transforms organizational dynamics. By acknowledging the blessings received and expressing appreciation for the contributions of others, leaders can cultivate environments where individuals thrive, relationships flourish, and collective goals are achieved. In the tapestry of leadership, gratitude emerges as a foundational thread, weaving together the fabric of success and fulfillment.

Cultivating Resilience through Gratitude

The concept of a growth mindset has gained significant traction in personal and work development and goal achievement. I even wrote a short treatise on the subject in 2022.

Coined by psychologist Carol Dweck, a growth mindset is the belief that one's abilities and intelligence can be developed through dedication and hard work. It contrasts with a fixed mindset, which sees abilities as innate and unchangeable.

While cultivating a growth mindset is crucial for business success, gratitude is another powerful tool to enhance this mindset. Gratitude, the practice of acknowledging and appreciating the good in one's life, profoundly affects mental well-being and can significantly influence the development of a growth mindset.

The Power of Perspective: Linking Gratitude and Growth

Gratitude and a growth mindset may seem unrelated, but their connection becomes apparent upon closer examination. Both concepts involve a shift in perspective—one from fixed to growth and the other from lack to abundance. When individuals adopt a grateful mindset, they train their minds to see opportunities instead of obstacles and strengths instead of weaknesses. This shift aligns perfectly with the principles of a growth mindset, where challenges are viewed as opportunities for growth, and effort is seen as the path to mastery.

One of the hallmarks of a growth mindset is resilience—the ability to bounce back from setbacks and failures. Gratitude builds resilience by helping individuals reframe adversity as a learning experience. When faced with challenges, grateful individuals are more likely to focus on the lessons learned and the support they receive rather than dwelling on the negative aspects of the situation. This positive outlook enables them to persevere despite difficulties and maintain a growth-oriented mindset.

Central to the growth mindset concept is the belief in the power of effort and learning. Individuals with a growth mindset embrace challenges and view failures as opportunities for growth. Gratitude complements this mindset by fostering a love for learning and a curiosity about the world. When people approach their work life with appreciation, they are more open to new experiences and perspectives, enhancing their capacity for learning and development. They see each day as an opportunity to grow and improve, leading to continuous self-improvement and personal growth.

Gratitude and a growth mindset are potent forces for personal development and achievement at work. By embracing gratitude, we shift our perspective from lack to abundance, fostering resilience, enhancing learning, and strengthening relationships. When combined with a growth mindset, gratitude catalyzes continuous growth and self-improvement. By cultivating both, we unlock our full potential and create a life filled with meaning, fulfillment, and success at work and in our personal lives.

Gratitude, Money and Stewardship

"I've always believed that what we have in life is on loan from God, and we're meant to do right by it." ~John Wayne

---

L IKE MOST PEOPLE MY AGE, I have seen most of John Wayne's movies from, as a kid, in late 1950s, where his performances were accompanied by the smell of "punk" at a popular drive-in theater in Pasadena, Texas, to his version of *True Grit*, released on June 11, 1969, where he won his only Academy Award for Best Actor for his portrayal of Rooster Cogburn; to his final movie *"The Shootist*, released in 1976. In the film, Wayne plays J.B. Books, an aging gunslinger diagnosed with terminal cancer, reflecting parallels with Wayne's own life as he battled the illness. *The Shootist* is widely regarded as a fitting conclusion to his illustrious career, combining legacy, mortality, and honor themes. His statement, "I've always believed that what we have in life is on loan from God, and we're meant to do right by it," reflects a profound view shaped by his evolving faith, experiences, and a growing sense of responsibility. Known for his rugged screen persona and larger-than-life presence, Wayne's later years revealed a man who deeply considered the spiritual weight of his actions. His sentiment points to the understanding that life's material blessings, talents, and opportunities are not inherently owned but entrusted to individuals by God, requiring stewardship marked by integrity and humility.

Wayne's perspective on stewardship aligns with his gradual embrace of Christian values, particularly in the 1970s when he became more vocal about his faith. The actor, who portrayed stoic heroes and moral leaders in films, began to see his real-life role as a steward of influence. He used his celebrity status to highlight duty, gratitude, and compassion themes. His philosophy mirrored biblical teachings such as Matthew 25:14-30, we discuss further in this chapter, where the parable of the talents emphasizes accountability for the gifts and resources given by God. Wayne's view also resonates with the idea that wealth, power, and opportunity are not measures of personal success but tests of character. By "doing right by it," Wayne advocated using such blessings to benefit others, leave a meaningful legacy, and honor the divine source of all life's gifts.

In a broader sense, it appears to me that Wayne's statement challenges the cultural tendency to view success as a personal accomplishment rather than a spiritual responsibility. It suggests a shift from individualism to interconnectedness, where blessings are considered part of Godly trust, requiring careful and thoughtful stewardship. For Wayne, this belief represented not just a personal mantra but a guiding principle that shaped his later years, leaving behind a legacy of humility, faith, and purpose that continues to resonate to this day in many corners of even our natural life.

In the late 1990s, I had just moved back to Houston from Santa Fe, New Mexico, coming out of retirement for the first time, to start a building company partnering with a homebuilder out of Phoenix, Arizona. Our focus in New Urban Homes was on the vibrant Museum District of Houston. JD was a young man trying to find his way in the world. I had known JD, the son of an old horse trainer and professional rodeo clown buddy from the early 1980's. I knew him when he was knee-high to a grasshopper, always reaching for the stars with big dreams and a competitive spirit that drove him to outdo everyone around him. We crossed paths here after about fifteen years when I was starting an exceptionally large seven story residential project in the District. Even back then, JD stood out—an ex-Marine with a determined spirit, eager to make his mark.

I know some of JD's story from his dad, whom I had kept in touch with over the years, and after leaving the military, JD had always been drawn to the thrill of the rodeo, where he could channel his restless energy into something tangible. He became a bull rider, known for his courage and resilience. But the rodeo circuit took its toll on JD, and after a particularly rough ride, he suffered a serious back injury. The injury was severe enough to force him to leave the rodeo, and it dogged him for years, a constant reminder of the risks he had taken.

Despite the pain and the end of his rodeo career, JD was not the kind of man to let setbacks define him. He turned to construction, just as I had seen others do in Houston as the downtown urban home-building cycle had been born again in the mid-1990s.

Starting small, he used the same grit that had carried him through the Marines and the rodeo to build a commercial renovation and construction business from scratch. His reputation grew quickly in the community—people trusted JD because he was a man of his word. As his business expanded, he became known for the quality of his work and the integrity with which he conducted himself.

While visiting a neighboring site one day, I ran into JD and struck up a conversation. We talked about the challenges of the business, the pressures of being responsible not only for oneself but for a team of workers, and the weight of financial success. Despite his accomplishments, I could sense that JD was grappling with something more profound. He had all the markers of success, but there was a void he could not fill.

I remember suggesting to JD that he meet with Reverend Eli Turner, a pastor for a church in the 3rd Ward of Houston who had a knack for helping young men of color find clarity in their lives. JD took the advice, and he and the reverend developed a friendship over time. Reverend Turner introduced JD to the Parable of the Talents, a story that spoke directly to JD's struggles. What you have been given to make a positive impact resonated deeply with him.

As Reverend Turner recounted how a master entrusted his servants with talents—coins of great value—JD began to see his life in a new light. The parable's lesson about stewardship was that his success was not just a personal achievement; it was a responsibility, a divine trust.

Soon after, JD began to reframe his approach to business. He started to see his work as more than just a way to earn a living; it became a means to serve others and to honor the blessings he had received. He began to invest in community projects, fund scholarships for young people, and look for ways to give back, all while asking himself, "How can I steward this for the greater good?"

During one of these community endeavors, JD met Sara, a woman whose faith and kindness captivated him. Sara was volunteering at a local shelter that JD had been helping to renovate, and their connection was immediate. As they spent more time together, JD realized he could not imagine his life without her. They married not long after, and a year later, they were blessed with a beautiful daughter, Grace.

With Sara by his side and Grace in his arms, JD's life took on a new dimension. His gratitude deepened, and he found peace that had eluded him for years. He was no longer driven by the need to prove himself but by a desire to be a faithful steward of the life and love he had been given.

The back injury that had once been a source of pain and frustration now served as a reminder of how far he had come. Jake had learned to live with the pain, but more importantly, he had learned to focus on the blessings that life had brought him. He knew that his journey from the rodeo to construction, from injury to healing, had shaped him into the man he was meant to be.

One evening, as I visited JD in his home, I saw a man who had truly found his place. The sun was setting over Houston, casting a warm glow over the city, and JD was content. He had renovated more than just homes—a life filled with purpose, love, and gratitude. As we sat there, he shared a realization that had come to define his approach to life:

"Gratitude, money, and stewardship," JD began, "they are all connected in a way I never fully understood before. Money isn't just something we earn or spend; it's a tool, a power that we are entrusted with. How we use it reflects our values and our faith. The Parable of the Talents gave me a model to understand that. It's not just about holding on to what we have; it's about growing it, using it wisely, and making sure it serves a greater purpose."

He paused his gaze thoughtful, "Gratitude has transformed how I view money. It is not about possession anymore, it's about stewardship. I have learned to use my resources not just to build a business, but to serve others, to contribute to God's work, and to build relationships that have eternal value. Budgeting, saving, investing, generosity—those are not just financial principles; they're ways to honor God with what He's given us."

JD looked at me, and I could see the depth of his conviction. "Money isn't ours to possess. It's the power to be stewarded with integrity and gratitude. When we do that, we honor God, we reflect His character in our lives, and we use our resources to make a positive impact and advance His kingdom. That is the kind of legacy I want to leave behind."

As we sat there, the words of the Parable of the Talents echoed in my mind: "Well done, good and faithful servant." JD had truly embraced the biblical framework of financial stewardship, and in doing so, he had found a life of purpose, peace, and profound gratitude.

Money is often seen as a symbol of power, security, and success in our society. We work hard to earn, save, and invest, believing it holds the key to our happiness and fulfillment. Yet, from a biblical perspective, money is not ours to claim. It is a resource entrusted to us by God, and how we use it reflects our stewardship—a responsibility to manage God's resources in a way that honors Him. Here, I will explore the relationship between gratitude, money, and stewardship, focusing on the biblical principle that money is a tool of power and influence meant to be stewarded wisely. The Parable of the Talents will serve as a central scriptural reference, illustrating the importance of faithful stewardship and the consequences of effectively failing to use God-given resources.

The Nature of Money

"It is not our money; money is God given power and how you wield it is stewardship"
~Neil McClendon[7].

Money is a medium of exchange, a representation of value, and a means of facilitating transactions. However, beyond its economic function, money carries significant power. It can be used to build, bless, uplift, or be wielded destructively, leading to greed, corruption, and oppression. The power of money lies not in the currency itself but in how it is utilized by those who possess it.

The Bible is clear that wealth, like all things, comes from God. Deuteronomy 8:18 states, "You shall remember the Lord your God, for it is He who gives you the power to get wealth." This verse reminds us that our ability to earn money is a gift from God, which carries a responsibility. Money, therefore, is not an end but a tool that must be used according to God's purposes.

In the New Testament, Jesus speaks frequently about money and wealth, often warning against the dangers of loving money more than God. In Matthew 6:24, He says, "No one can serve two masters, for either he will hate the one and love the other, or you will be devoted to the one and despise the other. You cannot serve both God and money." This passage highlights the importance of placing God above material wealth and recognizing that money should serve God's purposes rather than becoming an idol in our lives.

Gratitude as the Foundation of Stewardship

Establishing a grateful mindset will reshape your viewpoint with money and resources. When we recognize that everything, we have is a gift from God, our perspective on money shifts from ownership to stewardship. Gratitude cultivates a mindset of thankfulness for God's provision and a desire to use our resources in ways that honor Him.

We have mentioned many times in this book that the Apostle Paul emphasizes the importance of gratitude in 1 Thessalonians 5:18, where he writes, "Give thanks in all circumstances; for this is God's will for you in Christ Jesus." This attitude of gratitude is not contingent on our financial situation but is a constant recognition of God's goodness and faithfulness. When we are grateful, we are less likely to hoard wealth or use it selfishly; instead, we seek to bless others as we have been blessed.

Gratitude also helps us to avoid the pitfalls of greed and materialism. In 1 Timothy 6:6-10, Paul warns, "But godliness with contentment is great gain. For we brought nothing into the world, and we can take nothing out of it. But if we have food and clothing, with these we will be content. But those who desire to get rich fall into temptation, into a snare, into many senseless and harmful desires that plunge people into ruin and destruction. For the love of money is the root of all kinds of evil. It is through this craving that some have wandered away from the faith and pierced themselves with many pangs." Here, Paul contrasts the dangers of loving money with the contentment that comes from godliness and gratitude. By cultivating a heart of gratitude, we guard against the destructive power of greed and instead focus on using our resources in ways that reflect God's love and generosity.

The Parable of the Talents

One of the most potent biblical stewardship teachings is the Parable of the Talents, recorded in Matthew 25:14-30. In this parable, Jesus tells the story of a man who goes on a journey and entrusts his wealth to his servants. To one servant, he gives five talents; to another, two talents; and to a third, one talent, each according to his ability. The first two servants invest their talents and double their master's money, while the third servant buries his talent in the ground out of fear.

When the master returns, he commends the first two servants for their faithfulness and rewards them with greater responsibilities. However, the third servant is rebuked for his laziness and lack of initiative, and his talent is removed. The parable ends with a sobering statement: "For whoever has will be given more, and they will have an abundance. Whoever does not have, even what they have, will be taken from them."

The Parable of the Talents is a profound lesson in stewardship. The talents in the parable represent the resources, opportunities, and abilities that God has entrusted to each of us. The master expects that his servants will use these gifts wisely and productively, not merely for their benefit but for the benefit of the master. In the same way, God expects us to use the resources He has given us—our time, talents, and money—in ways that advance His kingdom and reflect His character.

The third servant's failure is not in losing the master's money but in failing to use it. This underscores the importance of taking initiative and being proactive in our stewardship. God does not call us passive recipients of His blessings but active participants in His work. The reward for faithful stewardship is the return on investment and the opportunity to share in God's joy and be entrusted with even greater responsibilities.

Money as a Tool for God's Kingdom

When we view money through the lens of stewardship, we see it as a tool for advancing God's kingdom rather than a means of personal gain. This perspective shifts our priorities from accumulating wealth to using our resources to serve others and glorify God.

One way we can use money as a tool for God's kingdom is by practicing generosity. Proverbs 11:24-25 states, "One person gives freely, yet gains even more; another withholds unduly but comes to poverty. A generous person will prosper; whoever refreshes others will be refreshed." This principle of sowing and reaping is echoed throughout scripture, reminding us that generosity leads to blessing for the giver and the community.

The New Testament also encourages believers to give generously and sacrificially. In 2 Corinthians 9:6-7, Paul writes, "The point is this: Whoever sows sparingly will also reap sparingly, and whoever sows bountifully will also reap bountifully. Each one must give as he has decided in his heart, not reluctantly or under compulsion, for God loves a cheerful giver." This passage highlights the importance of giving with the right attitude—one of joy and willingness rather than obligation or guilt.

In addition to giving financially, we can use our money to support causes and initiatives aligning with God's purposes. This might include supporting missionaries, funding charitable organizations, or investing in projects that promote justice and mercy. By using our resources to further God's work in the world, we demonstrate our commitment to His kingdom and our trust in His provision.

Stewardship Beyond Money: Time and Talents

While money is an essential aspect of stewardship, it is not the only resource that God has entrusted to us. Our time and talents are equally valuable, something we must steward with the same care and intentionality.

At my age, time is a precious resource that, once spent, cannot be reclaimed. Ephesians 5:15-16 urges believers to "Look carefully then how you walk, not as unwise but as wise, because the days are evil." This passage reminds us that time is short and that we must use it wisely, prioritizing the things that matter most—our relationship with God, our families, our communities, and our service to others.

Stewarding our time well requires intentionality and discipline. It means setting aside time for prayer, worship, and studying God's word, building meaningful relationships, and serving those in need. It also means avoiding the distractions and timewasters that distract us from God's purposes.

Our talents and abilities are another area of stewardship. Romans 12:6-8 teaches, "Having gifts that differ according to the grace given to us, let us use them: if prophecy, in proportion to our faith; if service, in in our serving; the one who teaches, in his teaching; the one who exhorts, in exhortation; the one who contributes, in generosity; the one who leads, with zeal; the one who does acts of mercy, with cheerfulness." This passage reminds us that God has gifted us with unique talents and abilities and calls us to use them to serve others.

Stewarding our talents means recognizing that our abilities are not our own but are gifts from God, meant to be used for His glory. It means developing our skills, using them to bless others, and seeking opportunities to serve in ways that align with our God-given strengths.

Gratitude Mindset's Explicit Link

The biblical fiscal management framework intricately links gratitude, money, and stewardship. Money holds significant power as a tool; how we steward it reflects our values and faith. The biblical concept of talents provides a transparent model for understanding stewardship. We are entrusted with resources to be used wisely and productively, focusing on growth and faithfulness.

Gratitude transforms our approach to money from one of mere possession to one of purposeful stewardship. It encourages us to use our resources to serve others, contribute to God's work, and build relationships that have eternal value. By embracing the principles of budgeting, saving, investing, generosity, and avoiding debt, we can manage our finances in a way that honors God and fulfills our responsibilities.

As we navigate the complexities of financial stewardship, let us remember that money is not ours to possess but a power to be stewarded with integrity and gratitude. In doing so, we honor God and reflect His character in our lives, using our resources to make a positive impact and advance His kingdom.

Stock image by Getty Images

Gratitude & the Power of Realistic Expectations

> *"It's not dying I'm talking about; it's living... And knowing that you have limits and making sure you do the best with them." ~Robert Duvall[8] (from Lonesome Dove)*

I N LIFE, IT'S COMMON TO set goals, map out plans, and anticipate a future based on our hopes and expectations. Whether you are a top student at school or someone with detailed career plans, the idea that you can predict the future can be deeply ingrained. Yet, the reality is, life rarely turns out exactly as we expect it to. This disconnect between expectation and reality often leads to disappointment, frustration, or a feeling of failure. But gratitude's an often-overlooked factor that can help us manage these inevitable deviations from our plans.

Gratitude is not just about appreciating the good things in life; it is also about accepting and finding value in the unexpected. By adopting a grateful mindset, we can learn to manage and recalibrate our expectations, viewing life's surprises as opportunities rather than setbacks. This article will explore the connection between gratitude and having realistic expectations, demonstrating how gratitude can be a powerful tool in navigating life's unpredictability.

In the iconic movie *Lonesome Dove*, Robert Duvall masterfully portrays Gus McCrae, a retired Texas Ranger with an indomitable spirit, sharp wit, and a zest for life that captivates both his fellow characters and the audience. Gus's philosophy is summed up in his memorable quote, "It's not dying I'm talking about; it's living... And knowing that you have limits and making sure you do the best with them. This sentiment reflects the heart of his character; someone who embraces life fully, despite its challenges, and strives to find joy and purpose within his limitations.

The quote ties profoundly to the theme of gratitude. Gus's words emphasize the importance of acknowledging our human limits—not as constraints that diminish us, but as markers that guide us toward meaningful goals. To Gus, life is not about avoiding death; it's about making the most of the time we're given. This perspective fosters a sense of gratitude, urging us to focus on the richness of the present moment rather than the inevitability of life's end. Gratitude, in this context, is the acknowledgment of life's inherent value, even with its imperfections.

For modern audiences, Gus McCrae's philosophy offers a timeless lesson: life is not defined by the absence of challenges but by how we respond to them. By acknowledging our limitations and focusing on what we can control, we can live with a sense of purpose and fulfillment. Gratitude plays a vital role in this process, as it helps us shift our focus from what we lack to what we have, fostering resilience and optimism.

The Problem with High Expectations

We live in a culture that encourages us to set elevated expectations for ourselves. From an early age, we are often taught that if we work hard enough, we can achieve anything we want. While motivating, this message can also create an unrealistic sense of control over the future. Many students, for example, enter school believing that being at the top of the class guarantees success in life. However, real-world outcomes often show that top academic performance does not always translate into professional success.

You might know someone from your school days who did not perform as well academically but has gone on to start a successful business or climb the corporate ladder. The frustration that arises when you feel you have worked harder or deserve more than someone else can lead to resentment, disappointment, or even bitterness. Why did things not go according to plan? Why does someone with less talent or ability get ahead?

This gap between what we expect and what happens can often create a cycle of dissatisfaction. But gratitude can be pivotal in reshaping our approach to life precisely here.

Life's Unexpected Turns

The world is unpredictable, and no amount of planning can account for all of life's variables. The top students may enter the workforce only to find that their academic prowess doesn't align with the demands of their industry. Someone with less schooling might succeed because of traits like resilience, adaptability, and a willingness to embrace opportunities. Life throws curveballs—unexpected job opportunities, sudden health challenges, relationship changes—and while we can influence our lives, we can never fully control it.

This reality can be difficult to accept. When things don't go as planned, we often react with frustration or disappointment. However, a keyway to navigate this uncertainty is to cultivate gratitude. Gratitude does not mean giving up on goals or settling for less, it means recognizing that even when things don't go as expected, there is still something to be gained.

The Role of Gratitude in Managing Expectations

When we adopt a mindset of gratitude, we shift our focus away from what we lack or what didn't happen according to plan and begin to appreciate what we have and can still be. This mental shift helps us realistically manage our expectations, making us more adaptable to life's inevitable twists and turns. Let's explore how gratitude can specifically help us handle life's unpredictability.

Gratitude Encourages Flexibility

Rigid expectations can lead to disappointment, but gratitude allows us flexibility. When life doesn't go according to plan, a grateful mindset helps us see alternate paths and opportunities we might not have considered. For example, if you are passed over for a promotion you worked hard for, it's easy to dwell on the unfairness of the situation. However, gratitude can help you focus on what you have gained from the experience—new skills, deeper insights, or even a better understanding of what you truly want.

Being grateful for the journey rather than fixated solely on the outcome allows you to adapt more easily when things don't unfold as expected. This flexibility is crucial in navigating life's inevitable surprises and detours.

Gratitude Shifts Focus from Comparison to Personal Growth

It's easy to compare ourselves to others, especially when we see people who seem less deserving to enjoy success. You've worked harder than a colleague, but they were the ones who got the promotion, or a former classmate who didn't perform well academically has gone on to launch a thriving business.

These comparisons are often frustrating, but gratitude helps us reframe our thinking. Instead of focusing on what others have that we do not, we can be grateful for our journey, acknowledging the unique lessons, skills, and experiences we've gained. Gratitude shifts the emphasis from competition and comparison to personal growth, reminding us that each person's path is different.

Gratitude Helps Us See Setbacks as Opportunities

One of the most powerful aspects of gratitude is its ability to reframe setbacks as opportunities. When you adopt a grateful mindset, you begin to view challenges not as roadblocks but as stepping-stones. For example, losing a job might seem like a disaster. Still, with a grateful perspective, it could also be an opportunity to pursue a passion, learn a new skill, or even take a well-needed break to reassess your priorities.

Gratitude helps us see that life's surprises- both good and bad—are part of the journey. By focusing on what we can learn and how we can grow from these experiences, we can turn even the most difficult situations into opportunities for development.

Gratitude Reduces Stress and Increases Resilience

Managing expectations is a significant source of stress for many people. The emotional toll can be overwhelming when things do not go as planned. However, gratitude has been shown to reduce stress and increase resilience. Focusing on the positives— no matter how small —can help us better cope with challenges and setbacks.

For instance, someone facing financial difficulties might initially feel defeated. However, they can maintain a more optimistic and resilient outlook by practicing gratitude for what they still have— whether it is supportive family members, good health, or opportunities to learn. This mindset can give them the strength to push through tough times and become more assertive on the other side.

Gratitude Enhances Our Ability to Stay Present

Another way gratitude helps us manage expectations is by grounding us in the present moment. Often, our expectations are tied to the future—what we want to happen, what we think should happen—but gratitude brings us back to the here and now. When we are grateful for what we have, we're less likely to get caught up in what might happen down the road.

This doesn't mean we shouldn't plan or set goals, but rather that we should appreciate the present moment, regardless of whether our plans are unfolding as expected. By staying present, we can appreciate the journey rather than being overly focused on the destination.

Realistic Expectations and the Balance with Ambition

It's important to clarify that realistic expectations don't mean lowering your ambitions. On the **contrary, it's about balancing, striving for excellence** and accepting that life won't always go according to plan. Gratitude is the tool that allows us to maintain this balance. It helps us pursue our goals passionately while also being open to the unexpected opportunities life presents.

Many successful people didn't achieve their goals as they originally envisioned. Some took completely different paths than they expected, and many of them credit their success to their ability to adapt to changing circumstances. They learned to be grateful for the detours, recognizing that those unexpected turns often led them to greater success than they had initially imagined.

Photo by Britta Pedersen-Pool/Getty Images

The Role of a Growth Mindset in Fostering Gratitude

> *"Failure is an option here. If things are not*
> *failing, you are not innovating enough."*
> *~Elon Musk*

MUSK'S EMBRACE OF FAILURE IN the above quote offers not only insights for innovation but also transformative lessons for personal growth and the cultivation of gratitude. Often, the fear of failure prevents individuals from taking bold steps toward their goals or stepping outside their comfort zones. Whether it's launching a new business, mastering a challenging skill, or making a life-altering decision, the possibility of failure can be daunting. Musk's growth mindset challenges us to view failure not as an end but as a powerful teacher.

Reframing failure shifts the focus from outcomes to processes. Instead of asking, "What if I fail?" we can ask, "What can I learn if I fail?" This mindset fosters action, experimentation, and perseverance. Over time, it builds confidence and adaptability—traits that are indispensable for achieving personal and professional success. However, the impact goes deeper when we integrate gratitude into this approach.

When we view failure through the lens of gratitude, it transforms from a source of frustration to an opportunity for growth and reflection. Gratitude allows us to appreciate the lessons failure teaches us, such as resilience, problem-solving, and humility. Each setback becomes a moment to recognize the progress we've made and the strength we've gained, even in the face of challenges.

For instance, failing at a personal goal might initially feel disheartening, but gratitude can shift the perspective to one of appreciation for the effort invested and the insights gained. It reminds us to be thankful for the courage to try, the opportunity to grow, and the support systems—family, friends, or mentors—that guide us through difficult times.

Moreover, gratitude fosters optimism, which is essential for bouncing back from failure. By focusing on what we have learned and the resources we still possess, we can approach future challenges with renewed energy and hope. This positive outlook not only helps us recover but also motivates us to take on new risks and pursue meaningful endeavors.

Adopting Musk's mindset, paired with gratitude, creates a powerful cycle of growth. Each failure becomes a building block for success and a moment to reflect on the gifts inherent in the journey itself. Gratitude anchors us during challenging times, enabling us to see beyond the immediate pain of failure and recognize its long-term value.

Incorporating gratitude into the process of learning from failure enriches personal growth, making it not just about achieving success but also about finding joy and meaning in the journey. It helps us appreciate the progress we're making, the lessons we're learning, and the opportunities that lie ahead, no matter how challenging the path may seem. By doing so, we transform setbacks into steppingstones, building a life that's resilient, fulfilling, and deeply enriched by gratitude.

A growth mindset, coined by psychologist Carol Dweck, is the belief that our abilities, intelligence, and character can be developed through dedication, perseverance, and learning.

People with a growth mindset see challenges as opportunities, understand that failure is a step toward improvement, and welcome feedback as a chance to grow. When we embrace this mindset, we naturally cultivate gratitude and find deeper joy.

One of the hallmarks of a growth mindset is viewing challenges not as setbacks but as chances to learn and grow. When faced with difficulty, individuals with a growth mindset see value in the experience rather than focusing solely on the negative aspects. This perspective helps foster gratitude, allowing us to appreciate each hurdle as a building block to personal strength and resilience.

A robust biblical example of turning challenges into opportunities is the story of Joseph in the Book of Genesis.

Joseph faced challenges, beginning with betrayal by his brothers, who sold him into slavery out of jealousy. He was taken to Egypt, far from his family and the life he knew. Even there, after proving himself trustworthy, Joseph faced false accusations from Potiphar's wife and was imprisoned unjustly. Despite these trials, Joseph's faith in God never wavered, and he viewed each setback as an opportunity to serve and grow.

While in prison, Joseph interpreted dreams for two of Pharaoh's servants. This gift eventually led to an opportunity to interpret Pharaoh's troubling dreams, predicting seven years of abundance followed by seven years of famine. Joseph's insight and wisdom impressed Pharaoh, who appointed him second-in-command over Egypt. Joseph helped save Egypt and neighboring nations, including his family, through his leadership from severe famine.

Joseph later forgave his brothers and acknowledged God's hand in his journey. He told them, "You intended to harm me, but God intended it for good to accomplish what is now being done, saving many lives" Genesis 50:20 (NIV). Joseph's ability to view his trials as part of God's plan allowed him to turn his challenges into an opportunity for great good.

This story exemplifies how, through a growth mindset rooted in faith, even the most difficult circumstances can become opportunities to fulfill a larger purpose and cultivate gratitude for God's guidance.

Acknowledging the growth that comes from facing challenges, we see life's difficulties as gifts. This gratitude strengthens our resilience, fills us with a sense of purpose, and brings joy as we celebrate each step forward.

A growth mindset also changes our relationship with failure. Rather than viewing mistakes as indicators of inadequacy, individuals with a growth mindset see failure as a necessary step toward success. This outlook helps foster gratitude by encouraging us to appreciate each attempt, even if the result is not what we initially hoped for.

Another powerful biblical example of this time of embracing failure as a steppingstone to success is the story of Peter's denial of Jesus and his later restoration (found in Luke 22:54-62 and John 21:15-19).

In the Gospels, Peter, one of Jesus' closest disciples, experiences a profound failure when he denies Jesus three times on the night of Jesus' arrest. Peter's denial is a moment of personal failure and a profound betrayal of his faith and friendship with Jesus. After realizing what he has done, Peter is filled with regret and weeps bitterly (Luke 22:62). In this moment, Peter might have felt that he had failed beyond repair.

However, after His resurrection, Jesus lovingly restores Peter. In John 21:15-19, Jesus asks Peter three times if he loves Him, giving Peter a chance to reaffirm his commitment. Jesus does not dwell on Peter's failure; instead, He entrusts him with a new mission: "Feed my sheep." Through this experience, Peter becomes a more humble, compassionate, and effective leader.

Peter's story illustrates how failure can lead to spiritual growth and greater purpose. By embracing his failure, repenting, and accepting Jesus' forgiveness, Peter becomes a bold preacher of the Gospel, even facing martyrdom for his faith. His failure became a critical steppingstone to a deeper relationship with God and a life of impactful ministry.

By embracing failure as part of the growth process, we open ourselves to joy in all circumstances, appreciating each step on the journey. Gratitude blossoms as we realize that every attempt, no matter what the outcome, contributes to our ultimate success and shapes us into more robust, more capable individuals.

Embracing Feedback as a Tool for Personal Development

The Bible has a powerful story about appreciating feedback as a tool for personal development: the story of King David and the Prophet Nathan in 2 Samuel 12:1-13.

After David's wrongdoing with Bathsheba and arranging the death of her husband, Uriah, God sends Nathan to confront David. Nathan uses a story to illustrate the gravity of David's actions, leading David to realize his sin. Instead of reacting defensively or rejecting Nathan's message, David responds with humility and repentance, saying, "I have sinned against the Lord" (2 Samuel 12:13).

Though painful, David's acceptance of Nathan's feedback becomes a turning point for him spiritually. His humility and willingness to listen allow him to grow, seek forgiveness, and strengthen his relationship with God. This example demonstrates how accepting constructive feedback—no matter how difficult—can lead to transformation and growth.

David's response shows a growth mindset. He sees the feedback as a pathway to becoming a better person and a more faithful servant of God. Through this willingness to receive correction, David models how humility and gratitude for guidance can be personal and spiritual development tools.

Feedback can sometimes be challenging to accept, particularly if it's critical. However, a growth mindset invites us to view feedback as a tool for personal development. When we adopt this perspective, we become more grateful for the insights and guidance others provide, understanding that constructive feedback is essential for growth.

Another example is my mother, Irene Francis (Franny) Tousignant, who is now deceased, an accomplished artist and the chief color technician for Eastman Kodak and the NASA effort beginning in the mid-1960s. Kodak teamed up with NASA on space science and remote sensing missions for over 40 years, starting from this time.

When John Glenn became the first American to orbit the earth, as NASA's photographic contractor, Kodak was deeply involved in testing cameras and film stock to confirm they could endure space travel. Kodak worked with NASA engineers to assess equipment durability and suitability for high-speed launches, atmospheric reentry, and varying temperatures. This involved rigorous quality control and frequent equipment modifications based on spaceflight's unique challenges. Once the film returned from Glenn's mission, Kodak, under Franny's supervision, was charged with developing and processing it to ensure the images were preserved. Her experience in film development and archiving provided NASA with a reliable means to secure and manage these historic photographs. Kodak's processing standards ensured that the iconic images, including Glenn's views of Earth, were crisp, detailed, and true to the colors Glenn witnessed in space.

During the twenty-five years that Franny served as the top color technician for Eastman Kodak, her work environment was marked by an unrelenting pursuit of precision. Photography and algorithm standards constantly evolved, often sparking debate and friction. As a young man in my mid-30s, these critiques seemed like an attack on the process my mom diligently oversaw.

Sunday dinners at Mom's, where my brothers and I gathered weekly, were filled with stories from her workplace. Our instinctive reaction was to defend her against the perceived criticisms. But Franny saw things differently. She approached her work with a remarkable perspective: every critique, every change was not a slight but a gift. She often reminded us that feedback was an opportunity to refine her skills and achieve better outcomes. Her attitude transformed challenges into steppingstones and inspired her team to adopt a similar mindset.

This was long before the concept of a growth mindset gained prominence in popular psychology. Yet Franny embodied its principles. She understood that resilience and a commitment to learning were key to overcoming obstacles and achieving excellence. This approach not only defined her career but also earned her the highest recognition—at her retirement, Aron Cohn, then-director of NASA, commended her exceptional contributions to space photography.

Her legacy extended beyond her career. Even in her later years as a joyful grandmother, her gratitude for life and her belief in continual growth remained unshaken.

Gratitude and a growth mindset are deeply interconnected. Gratitude is the foundation that allows us to approach life's challenges with a sense of purpose and optimism. It enables us to see setbacks as opportunities to gain experience rather than as failures to fear. Born from this mindset, resilience strengthens our ability to navigate uncertainty and adversity with grace and peace.

When we embrace a growth mindset, we cultivate gratitude for every lesson learned, every challenge overcome, and progress made. This gratitude isn't tied to achieving perfection or specific outcomes—it arises from appreciating the growth journey. Living with this perspective transforms the way we experience the world. Challenges become opportunities, failures become lessons, and feedback becomes a path to refinement.

Franny's life stands as a testament to this powerful connection. By embracing challenges, valuing effort, and fostering continuous learning, she lived with a grateful heart and unwavering joy. Her legacy reminds us that true fulfillment lies not in perfection but in our gratitude for becoming the best version of ourselves. Through gratitude, we discover the joy of growth, and through growth, we nurture a life filled with purpose and meaning.

Roy Rogers & Dale Evens on horseback by Bettman/Getty Images

7 Habits for Building a Fulfilling, Interconnected, and Resilient Life

"It's the way you ride the trail that counts."
~Dale Evens[9]

MOST PEOPLE HAVEN'T YET DISCOVERED their grateful hearts. If you're one of them, don't worry—God installs one in each of us at birth. Embracing gratitude can profoundly change your perspective, allowing you to see the positive aspects even in challenging times. Sometimes, finding this gratitude takes years, even decades, and a fair share of tragedy. I know this because it took me seventy years and countless hardships to experience a glimpse of the effect of genuine gratitude. This shift in perspective transformed how I viewed my challenges and blessings, making me appreciate life's nuances more deeply. Even now, well past that defining moment, I'm still learning and growing in gratitude. But here's the incredible part: God places people in our lives to guide us.

Growing up in the 1940s (hopefully there are some reading this who also can reflect on this), I was captivated by *The Roy Rogers Show*. As a young viewer, I admired Roy Rogers, the "King of the Cowboys," and Dale Evans, the "Queen of the West." They seemed larger than life, riding horses and solving problems with a blend of courage, integrity, and grace. At the end of each show, Roy and Dale would sing "Happy Trails," a song that felt like a comforting farewell. I can still hear their warm voices harmonizing:

"Happy trails to you, until we meet again,
Happy trails to you, keep smiling until
then."

Back then, I didn't fully grasp the depth of their message, but now, many decades later, I understand it was more than a cheerful goodbye. It was a philosophy rooted in gratitude, faith, and perseverance—values Dale Evans exemplified in her life and work.

Dale once said, "It's the way you ride the trail that counts," a profound reflection on how we navigate life's challenges. It's not about the smoothness of the path but the attitude we bring to the journey. As a devout Christian, Dale believed that faith and gratitude were central to riding life's trail well. She shared this belief in her many books, which offered wisdom on overcoming adversity and finding strength through faith.

Reflecting on Dale's quote, I now realize it's a lesson we can all embrace. Life rarely unfolds as planned. We face detours, obstacles, and heartaches. Yet, as Dale demonstrated, the measure of our journey lies in how we respond—with gratitude, resilience, and faith.

Several years ago, as I navigated the complexities of parenting and nurturing a new marriage in my retirement, I met Diane, the wife of one of my closest friends. Diane's profound grace and deep-seated faith had a transformative impact on my life. A devout Christian, she champions the power of gratitude to forge and deepen relationships. She consistently aims to enhance the lives of those she advises, leaving a lasting imprint of positivity and healing.

In the late 2000s, amidst personal turmoil following the loss of my son's mother in 2009, I found myself a widowed father, burdened with doubt and anxiety about my capability to guide my son into adulthood. At this time, Diane's wisdom became a beacon for me. Our initial encounter when I was 75 and wrestling with launching my 19-year-old son into his own life marked the beginning of an informal yet profound therapeutic journey. Diane approached me with compassion, encouraging a newfound appreciation for the life and experiences God had granted me. This perspective seeded trust in my son's ability to carve out his own success or learn from failure.

Diane's gratitude-centric philosophy reshaped my outlook and permeated her wider community. She fostered a network of support and belonging, emphasizing the therapeutic power of connections and mutual support. Her efforts have consistently promoted healing, hope, and a sense of wholeness among those she engages in.

As Diane continues her mission, her dedication to spreading gratitude endures. Her empathy, optimism, and communal approach transform lives, guiding individuals toward recovery and gratitude. At the heart of Diane's influence lies a deeper concept: her grateful heart does not merely reflect thankfulness for the blessings in life; it actively produces a ripple effect of healing and connection. She shows us that gratitude is not just a fleeting feeling but a practice that can be cultivated even amidst life's struggles. By observing her actions, we learn that gratitude involves opening ourselves to others, listening with compassion, and finding purpose in our shared experiences. Diane teaches us that when we adopt a mindset of gratitude, we not only enrich our lives but also become vessels of hope and restoration for those around us. In this way, Diane's life is a powerful reminder that a grateful heart can be a source of endless strength and transformation.

If you do not live a life of gratitude now, there is no need to worry. The good news is that you can learn appreciation and develop a grateful mindset.

Most people do not have a problem expressing gratitude when things are going well for them. However, they do not think about expressing gratitude when having a wrong time or facing a crisis.

It is essential to emphasize that gratitude is a state of mind and a grateful mindset, nothing more than that. This is good news, as it means that with a change of perspective, you can find a good reason to be grateful even when everything around you seems to be falling apart.

It doesn't matter how bad things appear; you can always be thankful for something. Always remember that we are here for a brief time. We can readily appreciate this if we are alive and breathing.

When things go wrong in your life, which everyone must face from time to time, with a grateful mindset, you will always believe that things will improve. If you know someone with a thankful attitude, watch how they conduct themselves. You will soon start to see several common themes and behaviors.

Habit 1: Keep a Gratitude Journal

When you make it a habit of keeping a daily gratitude journal, you enter a mindset shift that can profoundly transform your mental, emotional, and even physical well-being. It's not just about counting blessings but actively re-wiring your brain to focus on the positive aspects of life. Recording daily moments of gratitude fosters more profound joy, resilience, and a more positive outlook, even during life's inevitable challenges.

Gratitude journaling can take many forms, from structured morning rituals to spontaneous reflections at the end of the day. Sitting down to reflect on what you're thankful for can also serve as a spiritual practice, enhancing your connection to God.

The Science Behind Gratitude

As I said earlier, research has consistently shown that gratitude significantly impacts mental health. Studies have found that people who regularly engage in gratitude practice, such as journaling, report higher levels of happiness, less depression, and increased feelings of connection to others. Gratitude is associated with improved sleep, lower blood pressure, and a strengthened immune system.

What happens when you make journaling gratitude a daily habit? It reshapes your brain. Neuroscience reveals that gratitude can help develop new neural pathways, reinforcing a more optimistic and resilient mindset. Writing down what you're thankful for amplifies these pathways, making it easier to default to gratitude in challenging situations. Over time, you develop a mindset that notices the good rather than getting bogged down by negativity or challenges.

Starting and maintaining a daily gratitude journal can initially seem daunting, but the benefits far outweigh the effort. With consistent practice, you will find that even the smallest moments—a warm cup of coffee, a kind word from a stranger, or a sunny day—can bring immense joy and fulfillment. As you write about these moments, you begin to build a repository of positivity. On difficult days, revisiting your past entries can remind you of the abundance in your life, helping you regain perspective and lift your spirits.

When practiced regularly, gratitude in journaling cultivates contentment. Life rarely goes according to plan, and challenges are inevitable, but daily giving thanks allows you to manage these moments with grace and perspective. This habit counterbalances a world that often encourages dissatisfaction or comparison. Instead of focusing on what's lacking, gratitude shifts your attention to what's already present and abundant.

Three Types of Gratitude Journals

While a simple notebook and pen can suffice for journaling, there are several ways to structure your gratitude practice, each with unique benefits. There are three types of gratitude journals, including one focused on morning prayer.

The Morning Prayer Journal: Giving Thanks for Life: The best way to begin the day is with prayer and reflection, thanking God for the gift of life. This type of gratitude journal is deeply spiritual, involving writing and a sacred conversation with God. In this journal, each entry starts with a prayer of thanksgiving, acknowledging God's goodness and grace.

A morning prayer journal might include thanking God for the ability to experience a new day, the strength to face its challenges, and the love surrounding you. By focusing on God's blessings at the very start of your day, you align your heart with His purpose and cultivate a spirit of humility and trust. This morning practice is about gratitude for the big and insignificant things—like the sunrise, the air you breathe, or the loved ones in your life.

Through this form of gratitude journaling, your relationship with God deepens, and you learn to see His hand in all aspects of your life. Gratitude becomes more than a momentary feeling; it transforms into a way of being, guiding your thoughts, actions, and reactions throughout the day.

The Five-Item Evening Journal: Ending the Day with Gratitude: The five-item evening journal is a structured practice that lists five specific things you are grateful for each night before bed. This form of journaling is perfect for those who want a simple yet powerful way to wrap up their day positively. By focusing on gratitude before sleep, you also encourage a sense of closure and peace.

The items you list can range from momentous events to minor, everyday pleasures. The key is specificity: instead of writing, "I'm grateful for my family," you might write, "I'm grateful for the conversation I had with my sister today, which brought me joy." This specificity helps you connect deeply with the emotions tied to each moment, enhancing the sense of gratitude.

Over time, this practice improves your emotional well-being and aids in better sleep, as you end each day with positive reflections instead of worries or stressors.

The Gratitude Letter Journal: Fostering Connection: Another powerful form of gratitude journaling is the gratitude letter journal. This involves writing letters of thanks to specific people— whether they are still living. These letters don't have to be sent, though they can be if you choose; even emailed or handwritten mailed letters are beautiful. The act of writing the letter itself can be healing and transformative, helping you express appreciation for the people who have made an impact on your life.

Each entry in this journal could be dedicated to a different person. For example, you might write a letter to a mentor who guided you in your career, a friend who supported you during a tough time, or even a relative who passed away but left behind cherished memories. The beauty of this type of journal is that it fosters deep reflection on relationships and connections.

By expressing gratitude to others, you also deepen your empathy and compassion. This practice shifts your focus from what others have done wrong to what they have done right, leading to more harmonious relationships and greater personal fulfillment.

Habit 2: Express Gratitude to Others

"Therefore encourage one another and build each other up, just you are doing." ~1 Thessalonians 5:11

Paul's words to the Thessalonians highlight the importance of encouraging and uplifting one another. Expressing gratitude is one of the simplest yet most profound ways to promote others, affirming their worth and contributions. This verse invites us to actively look for opportunities to build others up, creating an environment where gratitude becomes a shared habit.

Expressing gratitude to others is one of the most transformative habits anyone can adopt, which is the consistent practice of expressing gratitude to others. In a culture often focused on self-achievement, taking time to appreciate the people around us can seem secondary. However, expressing gratitude to others isn't just polite; it's a powerful habit that enriches our lives and the lives of those we acknowledge. This habit fosters deeper relationships, strengthens communal bonds, and profoundly enhances well-being. By consistently showing others, they are valued, we create a ripple effect of positivity that inspires and uplifts.

Expressing gratitude strengthens interpersonal bonds. According to research, people who frequently express gratitude have closer, more satisfying relationships with friends, family, and colleagues. It's a cycle of reciprocated kindness: the more we show appreciation; the more likely others will do the same. This builds trust and fosters an environment where people feel seen, valued, and motivated to contribute positively.

How to Cultivate the Habit of Expressing Gratitude to Others

Building a habit of expressing gratitude takes intentionality. Here are practical steps to make this habit a natural part of life:

Start Small and Be Specific: Begin by acknowledging the simple, everyday actions of those around you. Instead of just saying "thank you," add a reason—"Thank you for listening," or "I appreciate your diligence." Being specific enhances the sincerity of your gratitude and shows that you genuinely notice what they contribute.

Create Reminders: Life gets busy, and sometimes, gratitude can fall by the wayside. To prevent this, set up gentle reminders—whether a note on your desk, an alarm on your phone, or a calendar event—to prompt you to express gratitude to someone each day.

Express Gratitude Publicly: When appropriate, acknowledge someone's contributions publicly. This might mean expressing thanks in a team meeting or praising someone's work in a group email. Public acknowledgment strengthens the bond between you and the recipient and fosters a culture of appreciation.

Incorporate Technology Mindfully: In our digital world, sending a thank-you text or email can be as impactful as a handwritten note. Aim to be mindful and intentional with these messages, tailoring them to the person rather than using generic phrases.

The Impact of Expressing Gratitude on Personal Growth

Developing the habit of expressing gratitude to others cultivates a mindset of humility and openness. When we recognize the contributions of others, we are reminded that those around us often support our successes and joys. This habit shifts the focus from "I" to "we," nurturing a more interconnected and generous way of thinking.

Over time, regularly expressing gratitude can also build resilience. By appreciating our strengths and support systems, we learn to lean into relationships when faced with challenges. In turn, those we've acknowledged feel more motivated to support us during difficult times, knowing their efforts are valued.

The Ripple Effect: Inspiring Others to Adopt the Habit

Gratitude is contagious. When we show appreciation, others feel encouraged to adopt the same mindset. Whether a simple thank you or a heartfelt acknowledgment, each act of gratitude invites others to pause, reflect, and express thanks. This ripple effect strengthens communities and encourages a commitment to kindness, empathy, and support.

Imagine a workplace, family, or community where gratitude is a standard practice. Such an environment fosters trust, cooperation, and a sense of belonging. By making gratitude visible, we inspire others to recognize and celebrate their connections, creating a collective atmosphere that prioritizes mutual appreciation. "I do not cease to give thanks for you, remembering you in my prayers." Ephesians 1:16. The Apostle Paul frequently expressed gratitude for others, especially in his letters to early Christian communities. In Ephesians, he reminds readers of the importance of praying for and giving thanks to God for others. This verse illustrates how expressing gratitude for others can strengthen spiritual bonds and foster community and encouragement.

Incorporating the habit of expressing gratitude to others is not just about being polite. By taking time to acknowledge the impact others have on our journey, we deepen relationships and reinforce a sense of shared humanity. A grateful life isn't lived in isolation but thrives through recognizing, honoring, and uplifting those around us. As we cultivate this powerful habit, we discover that the path to gratitude is a path of connection, generosity, and mutual support.

Habit 3: Set Realistic Expectations

Developing realistic expectations is one of the most powerful habits for living a grateful life. Many of us are accustomed to setting grand goals and visions for our future, which can be inspiring but may also lead to disappointment if not balanced with practicality. Realistic expectations don't mean aiming low or giving up on big dreams; instead, they involve aligning our aspirations with the realities of life's unpredictability. By building this habit, we can foster gratitude, embrace resilience, and live a more peaceful, satisfied life.

When we cultivate realistic expectations, we create space for gratitude to thrive. Unrealistic expectations often lead to disappointment and frustration when things don't turn out as imagined. On the other hand, realistic expectations allow us to appreciate what unfolds and find value in outcomes we may not have initially planned. This mindset transformation—enjoying life's surprises—helps us grow in gratitude. Instead of feeling let down, we see life's challenges as steppingstones to personal growth and fulfillment.

Reverse-Engineering Goals from the Perfect Outcome

A powerful way to develop realistic expectations and build a grateful mindset is by reverse engineering your goals, starting with an ideal end state or desired outcome. A perfect end state is a vision of what your goal would look like if everything went perfectly. Imagine this vividly, including the emotions, achievements, and relationships involved. For instance, if your goal is to achieve financial independence, envision how it would feel, what your daily life would involve, and who would be around you in this ideal end state.

After defining your ideal outcome, reverse-engineer it by breaking down the steps needed. By working backward from your goal, you can identify realistic actions and set achievable milestones. Along the way, you may recognize that certain aspects of your ideal outcome may need adjustment, leading to a more attainable vision.

As you reverse-engineer your goal, it is essential to accept that life might introduce unexpected turns. These adjustments are not failures but necessary adaptations that bring us closer to a realistic version of our aspirations. By allowing space for these shifts, we cultivate resilience and foster gratitude for our progress, no matter how different it may be from the original vision.

Building The Habit of Setting Realistic Goals

To make realistic expectations a habit, set aside time to revisit and adjust your goals regularly. Reflect on how close you are to your desired outcome and whether it aligns with your current values and circumstances. By periodically re-evaluating your expectations, you can ensure they remain achievable and rooted in gratitude, guiding you to live a more fulfilling, interconnected, and resilient life.

Through cultivating realistic expectations, reverse-engineering our goals, and embracing life's unpredictability, we pave the way for a gratitude-centered approach to life that welcomes growth, resilience, and authentic fulfillment.

Habit 4: Practice Generosity with Joy and Purpose

To fully embrace generosity as a central habit, it's essential to understand the foundational perspective that money is not merely a personal asset, but a divine tool entrusted to us for advancing God's purposes. This perspective requires a significant shift in mindset—from seeing money as something to hoard or wield for personal satisfaction to viewing it as a means of service, ministry, and transformation.

A New Lens for Money

The Bible provides a clear framework for understanding financial stewardship. Scriptures like Matthew 6:19-21 teach us, "Do not lay up for yourselves treasures on earth, where moth and rust destroy and where thieves break in and steal, but lay up for yourselves treasures in heaven, where neither moth nor rust destroys and where thieves do not break in and steal." This passage reminds us that earthly wealth is fleeting and encourages us to invest in eternal values—relationships, acts of kindness, and advancing God's kingdom.

When we approach money with this eternal mindset, it transforms our priorities. Rather than striving for more significant bank accounts or luxurious lifestyles, we begin asking questions like:

How can my financial resources help those in need?

How can I contribute to spreading the Gospel?

What can I do to ensure my spending reflects my faith?

This perspective makes money a tool for doing good, empowering us to approach generosity with a joyful heart.

Generosity as an Expression of Faith

Generosity is not just about giving—it's an outward expression of our trust in God and gratitude for His provision. Giving freely demonstrates that we believe in God's promises to provide for us and meet our needs.

Proverbs 11:24-25 encapsulates this principle: "One gives freely yet grows all the richer; another withholds what he should give and only suffers want. Whoever brings blessing will be enriched, and one who waters will himself be watered." This verse teaches us the counterintuitive truth of God's economy: generosity leads to abundance, not lack. While the world often operates under a scarcity mindset, God calls us to live with open hands and hearts, trusting that He will replenish what we give.

Practicing Joyful Generosity

The Apostle Paul emphasizes the importance of the attitude behind giving in 2 Corinthians 9:6-7: "Remember this: Whoever sows sparingly will also reap sparingly, and whoever sows generously will also reap generously. Each of you should give what you have decided to give, not reluctantly or under compulsion, for God loves a cheerful giver."

Cheerful giving is grounded in gratitude. When we recognize all God has given us—salvation, provision, and countless blessings—we are moved to provide out of love and appreciation rather than obligation. To cultivate this habit, consider the following practical steps:

Reflect on God's provision: Spend time journaling or praying about how God has met your needs in the past. Recognizing His faithfulness fosters a grateful and generous heart.

Set giving goals: Decide in advance how much you want to give, whether it's a percentage of your income or a specific amount for charitable causes. Planning ahead makes generosity intentional.

Involve your family: Discuss giving with your spouse or children, making generosity a family value. Share stories of how your contributions make a difference, creating a sense of purpose and joy.

Making Giving a Regular Practice

Generosity becomes a habit when woven into your financial life. This might involve tithing—a biblical principle of giving the first 10% of your income to God's work—or it might take the form of regular contributions to charities, churches, or missions. The key is consistency.

Tithing holds a special place in Christian stewardship. In Malachi 3:10, God challenges His people: "Bring the full tithe into the storehouse, that there may be food in my house. And thereby put me to the test, says the Lord of hosts, if I will not open the window of heaven for you and pour down for you a blessing until there is no more need." This promise serves as both a challenge and an assurance: God blesses us in return when we give faithfully.

Beyond tithing, consider exploring other ways to give regularly:

Sponsor a child in need: Organizations like Compassion International or World Vision offer opportunities to provide ongoing support for children in poverty.

Contribute to local ministries: Support food banks, homeless shelters, or after-school programs in your community.

Create a giving fund: Set aside a portion of your monthly budget for spontaneous acts of generosity, such as helping a neighbor or responding to a disaster relief appeal.

Generosity Beyond Financial Giving

While financial giving is a significant aspect of generosity, it's not the only way to practice this habit. Sometimes, the most impactful gifts are time, skills, or a listening ear. Consider how you might:

- Volunteer at a nonprofit organization or ministry.

- Offer your professional expertise pro bono to someone in need.

- Share your home by hosting a small community group sponsored by your church or providing temporary shelter.

- Generosity is about a mindset of abundance, looking for ways to give freely and bless others with whatever resources you have.

Habit 5: Embrace Every Interaction with Confidence and Grace

A grateful mindset is a transformative way of viewing the world, characterized by an appreciation for life's blessings, even amidst challenges. One powerful habit of cultivating this mindset is to engage with everyone fearlessly. This approach opens the door to meaningful relationships, learning opportunities, and a deep sense of connection. Fearless engagement isn't about being reckless or aggressive; it's about setting aside judgments, embracing vulnerability, and approaching others with an open heart. Proverbs 27:17 (NIV) reminds us, "As iron sharpens iron, and one man sharpens another." This biblical wisdom underscores the value of interpersonal engagement in fostering growth and gratitude. Below, we delve into five practical ways to engage fearlessly and explore how they help promote a grateful mindset.

Start with Active Listening: Engaging fearlessly begins with active listening. When interacting with someone, focus entirely on their words, tone, and body language without planning your response. Giving your full attention demonstrates respect and builds trust, encouraging open communication.

For example, if a colleague shares a challenge, listen prematurely without interrupting or offering solutions. Instead, ask clarifying questions to understand their perspective better. This approach shows empathy, strengthens your connection, and often reveals insights you wouldn't have noticed otherwise.

Active listening fosters gratitude by deepening one's appreciation for others' experiences and perspectives. It shifts one's focus from self-centered concerns to a broader understanding of the world, enhancing one's sense of interconnectedness.

Practice Radical Acceptance: Fearless engagement requires radical acceptance—embracing people as they are without judgment or the need to change them. This doesn't mean agreeing with everything someone says or does but respecting their humanity and individuality.

If you encounter someone with differing political or cultural views, approach the conversation with curiosity rather than defensiveness. Seek to understand their perspective, even if you disagree. By doing so, you create an environment where both parties feel valued.

Accepting others fosters gratitude by helping you appreciate the diversity and richness of human experiences. It also reduces stress and conflict, allowing more positive interactions.

Offer Genuine Compliments: Offering genuine compliments is a simple but powerful way to engage fearlessly. Recognizing others' strengths or achievements—no matter how small—can brighten their day and strengthen your connection.

You might commend a barista for their cheerful service or praise a friend for their creativity in solving a problem. The key is sincerity; your compliments should come from a place of genuine appreciation.

Expressing gratitude for others' qualities encourages you to notice and acknowledge the good around you. Over time, this habit trains your mind to focus on the positives, building a grateful mindset.

Face Difficult Conversations with Courage: Fearless engagement includes addressing complex topics honestly and compassionately. Avoiding such conversations often leads to misunderstandings and unresolved tensions. By courageously facing them, you demonstrate respect for yourself and the other person.

If a friend's behavior has hurt you, have an open conversation about how you feel instead of harboring resentment. Approach the discussion with the intent to resolve, not blame.

When handled constructively, difficult conversations lead to growth and stronger relationships. They teach you to value honesty and vulnerability, key components of a grateful mindset.

Volunteer Your Time and Energy: Engaging fearlessly also means stepping outside your comfort zone to help others. Volunteering your time and energy—through formal programs or informal acts of kindness—is a tangible way to connect with people and make a positive impact.

Consider joining a community clean-up event, mentoring a young professional, or simply offering to help a neighbor with their groceries. These acts of service strengthen bonds and remind you of the value of community.

Serving others shifts your focus from what you lack to what you can give. It reinforces the abundance in your life and fosters a deep gratitude for the ability to contribute.

The Transformative Power of Fearless Engagement

Engaging with everyone fearlessly is more than a social skill; it's a transformative practice that reshapes how you view and experience the world. Here's why it's so effective in cultivating a grateful mindset:

Breaks Down Barriers: Fearless engagement helps you overcome biases, assumptions, and fears that often limit meaningful interactions. It fosters openness and authenticity, creating opportunities for deeper connections.

Builds Resilience: You develop emotional resilience by embracing vulnerability and stepping outside your comfort zone. This resilience helps you navigate life's difficulties with a grateful perspective.

Enhances Self-Awareness: Interacting fearlessly with others often holds up a mirror to your own beliefs, values, and behaviors. This self-awareness is crucial for personal growth and cultivating gratitude.

Strengthens Relationships: Gratitude thrives in the context of strong, healthy relationships. Fearless engagement nurtures these bonds, creating a support system that enriches your life.

Encourages Positivity: When you approach others with respect, curiosity, and kindness, you are more likely to receive the same in return. This positive feedback loop reinforces a grateful attitude.

Practical Tips to Sustain the Habit

Developing the habit of fearless engagement takes time and effort. Here are some practical tips to sustain this practice:

Set Intentions: Begin each day to approach interactions fearlessly. Remind yourself that every person you meet has something valuable to teach you.

Reflect and Adjust: Take time to reflect on your interactions. Celebrate your successes and identify areas for improvement.

Practice Self-Compassion: Engaging fearlessly can be challenging, especially if you are naturally introverted or shy. Be kind to yourself and recognize that growth is a gradual process.

Seek Feedback: Ask trusted friends or mentors about your communication and engagement skills. Use their insights to refine your approach.

Stay Curious: Curiosity is a powerful antidote to fear and judgment. Cultivate a genuine interest in others' stories, ideas, and perspectives.

Cultivating a grateful mindset through fearless engagement is a habit that can enrich every aspect of your life. By listening actively, practicing radical acceptance, offering genuine compliments, facing difficult conversations, and volunteering your time, you open yourself to a world of connection, growth, and joy. These practices not only deepen your relationships but also help you appreciate the beauty and abundance of life. As you engage fearlessly with others, you will find that gratitude becomes a fleeting emotion and a steadfast way of being.

The Transformative Power of Fearless Engagement

Fearlessly engaging with others can profoundly reshape your mindset and cultivate gratitude in ways you never imagined. Here's how this habit makes an impact:

Breaking Comfort Zones: Stepping out of your comfort zone opens you to new experiences and connections. This courage enriches your life with opportunities for growth and discovery, helping you see the abundance beyond familiar routines.

Building Relationships: Every person you meet has the potential to inspire you, share wisdom, or bring joy. Fearless engagement builds relationships that provide countless reasons for gratitude.

Developing Empathy: Listening, helping, and seeking common ground nurture empathy, a cornerstone of gratitude. Empathy allows you to appreciate others' journeys and makes you more aware of your own blessings.

Fostering a Positive Feedback Loop: As you engage more openly, your gratitude grows, making you more willing to connect with others. This positive loop enhances your well-being and creates a fulfilling, interconnected life.

Inspiring Others: Your actions can inspire those around you to embrace gratitude and fearless engagement. Leading through example contributes to a ripple effect of positivity and connection.

Developing a grateful mindset is a lifelong journey; fearlessly engaging with others is one of the most powerful habits to cultivate. By starting conversations, practicing active listening, offering help selflessly, seeking common ground, and expressing gratitude, you embrace the richness of human experiences and the interconnectedness of life. Each interaction becomes a reminder of God's blessings and the abundance that surrounds you. As you integrate these practices into your daily life, watch your gratitude deepen, your relationships flourish, and your perspective on life transforms for the better.

Habit 6: Present an Optimistic Viewpoint

Developing a grateful mindset is rooted in adopting a powerful habit: presenting an optimistic viewpoint. This practice fosters resilience and enriches every aspect of life by allowing us to see challenges as opportunities and blessings in disguise.

Biblical Foundations of Optimism and Gratitude

The Bible offers profound examples of how optimism fueled by gratitude transforms lives. The Apostle Paul stands out as a shining illustration. Once a fierce persecutor of Christians, Paul experienced a life-altering encounter with Jesus on the road to Damascus. Following his conversion, he endured countless hardships, including beatings, imprisonment, and shipwrecks. Despite these trials, Paul's gratitude for God's grace and faithfulness kept his spirit unwavering.

Paul exemplified this mindset in his letter to the Philippians, written while in prison. He expressed profound appreciation for the support of the Philippian church, writing, "I thank God in all my remembrance of you" (Philippians 1:3). Paul's optimism was contagious as he encouraged believers to maintain joy and gratitude, famously stating, "Rejoice in the Lord always; again, I will say rejoice!" (Philippians 4:4). His ability to focus on God's provision and the encouragement of others fueled his optimism, even in dire circumstances.

Everyday Examples of Optimism Through Gratitude

The power of optimism fueled by gratitude extends beyond biblical examples into both historical and modern lives.

John Muir, the Scottish American naturalist, and early advocate for preserving wilderness, found his optimism in the natural world. His gratitude for the beauty of untouched landscapes inspired a lifetime of environmental advocacy, leaving a legacy of conservation that continues to shape the world today. For Muir, nature's magnificence was a constant reminder of life's wonder, which sustained his optimistic belief in humanity's capacity to preserve it.

A contemporary example is Elon Musk, the entrepreneur behind companies like SpaceX and Tesla. Musk has faced significant challenges, from near bankruptcy to repeated rocket failures. Yet, his relentless optimism fuels his gratitude for the opportunity to solve humanity's most critical challenges, such as climate change and space exploration. Musk's ability to focus on possibilities rather than setbacks exemplifies how gratitude can inspire an unshakeable belief in a brighter future.

The Link Between Gratitude and Optimism

People with a grateful mindset naturally develop a positive outlook on life. Gratitude shifts focus from what is lacking to what is abundant, enabling even minor victories to feel like monumental achievements. This perspective helps cultivate resilience, as optimism *empowers* individuals to navigate life's unpredictability with hope and joy.

Consider the difference between optimism and pessimism. Optimism energizes and inspires, while pessimism drains and demoralizes. By choosing gratitude, you welcome optimism into your life, making it easier to remain steadfast even when faced with challenges.

Practical Steps to Cultivate Optimism Through Gratitude

Start Small: Develop the habit of expressing gratitude for minor blessings, such as a kind word, a warm cup of coffee, or a sunny day. These moments of appreciation accumulate and reshape your mindset.

Reframe Challenges: Instead of dwelling on obstacles, focus on the lessons they offer or the opportunities they create. Gratitude allows you to find the unseen benefit in demanding situations.

Celebrate Small Wins: Acknowledge and celebrate incremental progress. Each small step forward is a reason for optimism and gratitude.

Surround Yourself with Positivity: Engage with people, books, and environments that uplift and inspire you. Optimism thrives in a supportive atmosphere.

End Profanity and Violence: Be mindful of the content you consume and the language you use. Avoid movies, podcasts, and conversations filled with profanity or violence, as these can subtly shape your mindset and make it harder to remain optimistic. Instead, choose entertainment and discussions that uplift, inspire, and reinforce gratitude and positivity.

By incorporating these practices into your life, you will cultivate an optimistic perspective that fuels a grateful mindset and enriches your overall well-being.

The Transformative Power of Gratitude-Fueled Optimism

As you integrate gratitude into your daily life, you will find that optimism becomes second nature. Challenges that once seemed insurmountable will become manageable, and life's uncertainties will no longer overwhelm you. Instead, you will approach each day with confidence, fueled by the belief that every moment holds potential for growth and joy.

By making gratitude a daily habit, you unlock a transformative power that shapes how you see the world and your place in it. This optimism improves your life and inspires those around you to adopt a more positive and hopeful perspective. Let gratitude lead you to a life filled with possibility and purpose.

Habit 7: Growth-Focused Courage: Transforming Struggles into Gratitude and Joy

A growth mindset, popularized by psychologist Carol Dweck[10], is more than a buzzword. It's a habit of continually choosing courage over comfort, possibility over limitation, and purposeful learning over passive resignation. Embracing a growth mindset means believing that your abilities, intelligence, and character are not fixed traits—they're capabilities waiting to be developed through effort, resilience, and reflection.

> *"Courage is being scared to death but saddling up anyway."* ~John Wayne

This quote encapsulates the very heart of a growth mindset. Rather than crumbling before obstacles, we learn to see them as invitations to grow. The fear we feel doesn't signal defeat; it invites courage. By taking up the reins and venturing forward—no matter how daunting the trailer, foster gratitude, appreciating the lessons learned, and the strength gained along the way.

When we adopt a growth mindset, we recognize that challenges spark growth, failures pave the path to improvement, and honest feedback illuminates new possibilities. This perspective doesn't just create better outcomes; it nurtures a grateful spirit. We start to feel thankful for every bump in the road, knowing each can propel us into higher levels of understanding, empathy, and achievement.

Below are principles and strategies for developing this essential habit and reaping the rewards of gratitude and joy.

Strategies to Cultivate a Growth Mindset Habit

Adopt a Learner's Journal: At the end of each day, reflect on a challenge you encountered. Write down what you learned, how you responded, and how you might approach it differently next time. Over time, you will develop a narrative of resilience and appreciation.

Redefine Failure: Instead of labeling a setback as a sign of inadequacy, reframe it as "learning data." Ask yourself: "What did this teach me? How can I use this information going forward?"

Seek Constructive Feedback: Actively invite trusted peers, mentors, or colleagues to give honest input. Rather than bracing for criticism, anticipate the growth it can inspire.

Practice Self-Compassion: Growth doesn't flourish under constant self-criticism. Treat yourself with kindness when you falter. Recognize that mistakes are part of the process and feel grateful for the resilience and insight they offer.

Set Incremental Goals: Instead of enormous leaps, aim for steady steps. Celebrate your gains, no matter how small. These ongoing acknowledgments build momentum, gratitude, and joy.

Developing a growth mindset is not a one-time decision but an ongoing habit—an evolving practice of courageously facing fears, warmly embracing new knowledge, and persistently moving toward better versions of ourselves. As we nurture this mindset, gratitude naturally follows. We begin to see the richness in our struggles, the value in our failures, and the gifts in our ongoing transformation.

By continually choosing to saddle up in the face of fear, we discover that life's difficulties can be great teachers. We become ever more grateful, resilient, and deeply joyful as we learn from these lessons.

Roping in Gratitude: Finding Focus, Faith, and Fulfillment in Life's Arena

> *"The horse is a mirror to your soul.*
> *Sometimes you might not like what you see.*
> *Sometimes you will. ~**Buck Brannaman**"*[11]

I N THE HUSTLE AND BUSTLE of modern life, it's easy to get caught up in the whirlwind of negativity. From the constant barrage of un-welcome news to personal challenges and setbacks, it can sometimes feel like the world is conspiring against us. Yet, amidst the chaos, there exists a powerful antidote – gratitude. Beyond just a fleeting feeling of thankfulness, gratitude has the potential to fundamentally transform our lives by changing our focus.

Life revolves around focus. What we focus on shapes our beliefs, attitudes, and experiences. If we constantly dwell on the negative aspects of life, it's no surprise that negativity has become our dominant reality. Problems seem insurmountable, and setbacks feel like the end of the road.

However, the converse is also true. By making it a habit to shift our focus towards gratitude, we open ourselves to a world of possibilities and abundance. This shift doesn't mean ignoring or denying the existence of challenges; instead, it involves reframing our perspective to find the silver lining in every situation.

Biblical wisdom offers insights into the transformative power of gratitude. In Philippians 4:8, the apostle Paul writes, "Finally, brothers and sisters, whatever is true, whatever is noble, whatever is right, whatever is pure, whatever is lovely, whatever is admirable—if anything is excellent or praiseworthy—think about such things." This passage underscores the importance of focusing on positive and uplifting aspects of life, which is at the heart of practicing gratitude.

I have followed the life of Dan "Buck" Brannaman since my years of riding well-trained trail horses in the Sandia Mountains of New Mexico and playing cowboy pickup polo on ranches all around Central Texas. I met him at one of his early clinics in Rio Rancho, NM in the early 1980s; learning that Buck Brannaman was brought up in the cowboy tradition of demanding work. A cowboy whose almost magical ability to calm unruly horses was an inspiration for the fictional 1998 Robert Redford movie The Horse Whisperer; the film reveals a man whose talent for training horses is rooted in a deeply traumatic childhood at the hands of an abusive father. A trauma that is better healed with a grateful mindset.

Brannaman understands that building trust and rapport with a horse is essential for effective communication and cooperation. The "Whisperer" fosters a positive relationship built on mutual respect by expressing gratitude for the horse's cooperation and understanding. He restores his own life, as he restores the life of the horse and as much, the owner's.

While Brannaman's teachings focus primarily on horsemanship, they often touch upon themes of gratitude and personal growth. For instance, he has expressed deep appreciation for the impact horses have had on his life, stating, "The horse saved my life, so that's kind of why I'll spend the rest of mine trying to help them."

Similarly, in our own lives, expressing gratitude fosters more profound connections with others and with ourselves. When we acknowledge and appreciate the kindness, support, and contributions of those around us, we strengthen our relationships and cultivate a sense of belonging. This shift in focus from what is lacking to what is abundant enhances our overall well-being and satisfaction with life.

In the adrenaline-fueled world of team roping, where my cowboy friend, and co-founder, Chairperson of the Lonestar Legacy Fund, Dan Welch, resides at the very top of his amateur status, success hinges not only on physical prowess and skill but also on mental fortitude and focus. Amidst the thundering hooves and the precise coordination between horse and rider, the mindset of the roper plays a pivotal role in achieving optimal performance. One often overlooked yet potent tool in this pursuit is gratitude – a force capable of transforming perspectives and enhancing outcomes in the sport.

Team roping, a quintessentially American rodeo event, involves two riders working together to rope a steer as quickly and efficiently as possible. Precision timing, seamless communication, and split-second decision-making are the hallmarks of this demanding discipline. However, beyond the technical aspects lies a deeper dimension where mindset and attitude intersect with performance.

Gratitude, as a practice and a mindset, holds the key to unlocking this more profound dimension. At its core, gratitude is more than just a fleeting feeling of appreciation; it is a transformative force that shapes how we perceive and interact with the world around us. By cultivating gratitude, Dan can shift his focus, enhancing their performance and overall well-being.

One of the fundamental principles underlying the efficacy of gratitude is its ability to change focus. In life, as in team roping, focus determines direction. Whatever we focus on becomes magnified in our consciousness, influencing our thoughts, emotions, and actions. If our focus is mired in negativity, we inevitably attract more negativity into our lives. Conversely, by adopting a grateful mindset, we redirect our focus toward the positive aspects of our experiences, thereby inviting more positivity into our lives.

Maintaining a positive focus is essential in the high-stakes arena of team roping, where split-second decisions can make or break a run. Gratitude is a powerful antidote to the pervasive negativity that can creep into ropers' minds amidst intense competition and pressure. Instead of dwelling on mistakes or setbacks, grateful ropers like Dan focus on the lessons learned, progress, and growth opportunities.

Moreover, gratitude fosters resilience in the face of adversity. Every roper encounters challenges and obstacles along the journey, whether a missed catch, a balky horse, or a tough break in competition. However, rather than succumbing to despair or frustration, a roper who has cultivated a grateful mindset approaches setbacks as opportunities for learning and development. They view each challenge as a steppingstone to tremendous success, recognizing that there is always something to be thankful for, even amid adversity.

At its core, gratitude is a conscious choice—a decision to shift our focus from what is lacking to what is abundant, from problems to possibilities, from despair to hope. However, like any skill, cultivating gratitude requires practice and persistence. It's not enough to simply acknowledge its importance; we must actively incorporate it daily.

Practicing gratitude involves more than counting our blessings; it requires a fundamental shift in perspective. Instead of dwelling on what we lack, we train ourselves to focus on what we have and what is going right in our lives. This shift in focus increases our sense of well-being. It opens us up to new opportunities and experiences we may have overlooked.

We have already recognized how important it is to cultivate gratitude through daily reflection and/ or journaling. Taking a few moments each day to write down three things we are grateful for can significantly impact our outlook on life. Whether it's a beautiful sunrise, a kind gesture from a friend, or a moment of inner peace, these reflections remind us of the abundance surrounding us.

Additionally, expressing gratitude to others is a powerful way to strengthen relationships and spread positivity. Whether through a heartfelt thank-you note, a simple act of kindness, or a sincere compliment, acknowledging the contributions of others reinforces a sense of connection and appreciation.

The transformative power of gratitude lies in its ability to change our focus and our lives. By directing our attention towards the positive aspects of life, we open ourselves up to a world of abundance, joy, and fulfillment. Whether through biblical wisdom, the gentle art of horse whispering, or the rugged resilience of a rodeo team roper, the message remains clear ---gratitude can transform our perceptions and experiences, one thankful thought at a time.

Better Quality of Life

In life's journey, we often find ourselves chasing after success, wealth, and relationships, believing they hold the key to our happiness and fulfillment. However, amidst pursuing these external markers of success, we often overlook the transformative power of gratitude. Cultivating a gratitude mindset can profoundly enrich our lives, enhance our well-being, and create a sense of contentment and peace. Drawing inspiration from biblical narratives and personal testimonies, we explore how a gratitude mindset can profoundly improve the quality of life.

In the book of Job, we encounter a narrative that delves into the depths of suffering and resilience. Job, a righteous and prosperous man, undergoes unimaginable trials and losses, including the devastation of his wealth, health, and family. Despite his profound suffering, Job maintains faith and expresses gratitude towards God. In Job 1:21, he declares, "Naked I came from my mother's womb, and naked shall I return. The Lord gave, and the Lord has taken away; blessed be the name of the Lord."

Job's story illustrates the transformative power of gratitude in the face of adversity. Despite his dire circumstances, Job finds solace in gratitude, recognizing the blessings bestowed upon him despite his trials. His unwavering gratitude is a beacon of hope, highlighting how a grateful attitude can sustain us through life's most challenging moments.

In the New Testament, we encounter the parable of the prodigal son, found in Luke 15:11-32. This parable tells the story of a young man who squanders his inheritance in reckless living, only to find himself destitute and longing for home. Upon his return, expecting condemnation, he is welcomed with open arms by his father, who rejoices at his homecoming.

The prodigal son's journey poignantly reminds us of the transformative power of gratitude and forgiveness. Despite his waywardness and mistakes, he is met with unconditional love and acceptance. His gratitude upon returning home reflects a profound shift in perspective, leading to reconciliation and restoration of familial bonds.

In my own life, I spent years chasing after material success and fleeting relationships, believing they held the key to fulfillment. Despite achieving external markers of success, I found myself plagued by a sense of emptiness and dissatisfaction. Multiple marriages and financial abundance failed to quench the deep longing within my soul.

However, everything changed when Jesus entered my life. Through His grace and guidance, I began recognizing the blessings hidden amidst the challenges and disappointments. Jesus surrounded me with Godly women whose love and support became indispensable pillars of strength. Their unwavering faith and kindness transformed my perspective, teaching me the invaluable lesson of gratitude.

As I embraced a gratitude mindset, I found my quality of life undergoing a profound transformation. No longer defined by material wealth or transient relationships, I discovered true fulfillment in the simple joys of everyday life. The love of my children, the beauty of nature, and the presence of God became sources of profound gratitude and contentment.

Through my journey, I learned that true abundance lies not in external possessions but in a heart filled with gratitude and love. My relationship with Jesus taught me that genuine wealth is found in relationships nurtured with kindness, compassion, and gratitude. Today, I am eternally grateful for the transformative power of a gratitude mindset, which has enriched my life beyond measure.

The power of a gratitude mindset is evident in biblical narratives and personal testimonies. From Job's steadfast faith to the prodigal son's transformative journey, we see how gratitude can transcend suffering, foster reconciliation, and restore hope. Likewise, in our own lives, cultivating a grateful mindset can lead to profound transformations, enhancing our well-being and enriching our quality of life.

As we journey through life's difficulties, we may never underestimate the transformative power of gratitude. In moments of abundance and adversity alike, may we echo Job's words, "Blessed be the name of the Lord," and cultivate a heart overflowing with gratitude. In gratitude, we find the key to true contentment, peace, and fulfillment in life.

The Gratitude-Fear Paradox

Another way gratitude changes your life is simply by making you feel happier. Studies have shown that being thankful is vital to feeling satisfied with your current circumstances.

The study asked the participants to write about a specific topic every week. While one group was asked to write about what made them unhappy, the other was asked to write only about what they were grateful for.

Meanwhile, a control group was asked to write about what had happened during the week without focusing on negative or positive elements. The result showed that the group that wrote about what they were grateful for felt more optimistic and happier about their lives than the others. This is because when we are feeling gratitude, we naturally feel comfortable as we begin to recognize what we have rather than what we don't.

Once you have practiced gratitude for a while, you'll recognize that it's easy to live in an appreciative state if you're grateful. Of course, it isn't always easy to achieve this. We all have our baseline of happiness. If we cross that threshold, one way or the other, we automatically become happy or unhappy. Yet, spend enough time developing a grateful mindset. You will spend more time on the positive side of that line rather than the opposing side.

One way gratitude can change your life is by reducing your fears. It's challenging to be both grateful and afraid simultaneously. Fear happens if you allow yourself to focus on the things that you cannot control. When you live in a fearful state, you end up dwelling on the worst-case scenario.

In the summer of 2009, my world shattered. I was sixty-five, the CEO of an award-winning home-building company I had co-founded, and the proud father of a bright, energetic six-year-old son. Life had always been a whirlwind of responsibilities and achievements. Still, nothing could have prepared me for the phone call that turned my life upside down. My wife, the loving mother of our son, was killed in a horrific car accident. In an instant, the foundation of our family crumbled.

For years, I had prided myself on my ability to juggle the demanding role of a CEO in an increasingly volatile market. The homebuilding industry was fraught with challenges, requiring my attention around the clock. I worked 80-hour weeks, driving the company forward. But as I stood in the emergency room that fateful afternoon, I knew I couldn't continue living the way I had been. My wife was gone, and my son needed me more than ever.

The days that followed were a blur of grief and confusion—the harsh reality of my new role as a single parent set in. I had to become a stay-at-home dad, a role I had never imagined for myself. The transition was terrifying. At the time, I had built my identity around my work, and now I was being forced to redefine myself in the wake of an unimaginable loss. The pressure was immense, and I questioned whether I could control everything to keep from losing everything.

Balancing my grief with the demands of parenthood was an overwhelming challenge. Every day felt like an insurmountable mountain. My son, too young to fully grasp the permanence of death, asked about his mother constantly. His innocent questions were like daggers to my heart, and I struggled to find the right words to comfort him while battling my despair. The weight of responsibility was crushing, and I feared I had failed at parenting and managing the remnants of my professional life.

One evening, as I was putting my son to bed, there was a knock at the door. It was my son's godmother, a dear friend of our family and best friend to my deceased wife. She had been a pillar of support since the accident, always ready with a kind word or a helping hand. That night, she brought more than comfort; she gave a lifeline. She handed me a small plaque with a prayer that would mean everything to me. It read: "God, grant me the serenity to accept the things I cannot change, the courage to change the things I can, and the wisdom to know the difference" (Niebuhr[12]).

I read the words aloud, their simplicity striking a chord deep within me. Tears welled in my eyes as I realized how much I had been struggling to control everything, to fix what was irreparably broken. The plaque's message became a mantra, a source of strength in the darkest times. I put it on my kitchen bar, where I could see it every morning and every night. Eventually, I had the words engraved on a pendant, which I wore around my neck as a constant reminder to this day.

As is known, the serenity prayer began to transform my perspective. I started to understand that things were beyond my control, and it was futile to exhaust myself trying to change them. My wife's death was a tragic, unchangeable fact. My grief was a process I had to go through, not something I could bypass or fix. However, I could change some aspects of my life, starting with how I approached my new role as a father.

I sought out support groups for single parents and widowers, where I found camaraderie and understanding. Sharing my story with others who had experienced similar losses helped lighten the burden of isolation. I began to focus on the aspects of parenting where I could be effective: creating a stable, loving environment for my son and ensuring he felt safe and cherished. I learned to let go of the need to be the perfect parent and instead aimed to be a present and loving one.

Gradually, I started to embrace my new reality with a grateful heart. Each day became an opportunity to create memories with my son and to witness his growth and resilience. I took joy in the small moments:

- Talking before bedtime about his school day
- Playing Nerf gun wars and hide and seek with his buddies in the backyard.
- Simply being there for him

These fleeting yet precious moments filled the void left by my wife's absence and began to heal.

Professionally, I made the difficult decision to step down as CEO. It was not an easy choice, but it was necessary. The company needed someone who could devote their full attention to its demands, and I needed to prioritize my family. This decision, guided by the wisdom of the serenity prayer, allowed me to focus on what truly mattered. Letting go of my role in the company was a humbling experience. Still, it also opened new possibilities for personal growth and fulfillment.

As time passed, I found that living with a grateful heart could change one's life. The tragic loss of my wife brought indescribable pain. Still, it also led me to a deeper understanding of what it means to live meaningfully. I learned to cherish the present moment, appreciate the people in my life, and accept the things I could not change. This shift in perspective brought a sense of peace and purpose that I had never known before.

My journey through grief and fatherhood has been a testament to the power of acceptance, courage, and wisdom. The plaque my son's godmother gave me was more than a simple gift; it was a beacon of hope. It guided me through the darkest times and helped me find my way to a place of gratitude. I now wear the words close to my heart, not just as a reminder of my struggles but as a symbol of the strength and resilience that emerged from them.

Yet, overcoming those fears is possible by developing a grateful mindset. If you become entirely thankful for all you have, even your problems, you will find very little space left for fear to occupy your mind.

When you are afraid of things, you no longer live in a state of abundance but in one of lack instead. Being grateful will put you back into that great state, instilling in you a belief that you are thankful for all you have now instead of worrying about the things you don't have right now and won't have in the future.

All too often, we tend to save all our gratitude for just a few select occasions, like holidays, birthdays, graduations, and other special moments. These days, we finally permit ourselves to feel thankful and, in turn, all the positive emotions and happiness that come with it. Instead, we should take that opportunity to question why we do not allow ourselves to feel this way every other day. Gratitude isn't just for special occasions; it can be for every day of the year.

Take the time to stop, think about what you must be grateful for, and genuinely appreciate it, regardless of the day of the week or year. By being more grateful daily, you can abolish much of the fear that drives your negativity. Decide to practice gratitude right now; your fears will slowly dissipate.

Life's Trials as Opportunities for Stronger Faith

I have known Kate for decades. She is a retired human resource executive and Santa Fe art gallery owner whose life story is impressive. With a warm smile reflecting the wisdom of the years well lived, Kate's journey is a testament to resilience, determination, grit, and gratitude.

Kate's life began humbly in Albuquerque, New Mexico, marked by the trials and triumphs that shape the human experience. As a young woman in the 1960s, she fulfilled her dream of becoming a Continental Airlines flight attendant (what they called them in the day) during the golden years when the airline was owned by Robert Six and his wife, Audrey Meadows.

After a couple of years, she left her dream job to follow a young investment banker she fell in love with while on a layover in Houston, Texas. They married and adopted a beautiful son four years later. Unfortunately, after 15 years, they called it quits. Though they remained close through the years, their son struggled with anxiety and self-identity for many years.

Years later, she embarked on an entrepreneurial journey alongside her second husband. Together, they ventured into various business endeavors, each a testament to their vision, hard work, and unwavering belief in their abilities.

Their path to success was not without its challenges. Kate's crippling guilt over the rejection of her son held her captive for years. They encountered setbacks, faced failures, and weathered storms that would have deterred many. Yet, through it all, Kate and her husband remained steadfast in pursuing their dreams, fueled by a grateful mindset that turned every obstacle into an opportunity for growth while continuing to help her son find his way.

Their perseverance paid off as they built and sold several businesses, reaping substantial profits. Their relentless dedication secured their financial future and afforded them a comfortable retirement, allowing them to savor the fruits of their labor in the twilight years.

However, amidst the accolades and achievements, Kate's heart longed for something more profound, a sense of purpose and fulfillment that transcended material success. It was during a period of introspection, soul-searching, and dealing with the guilt over her only son's rejection and tragic life that she found solace in her faith journey.

Through the highs and lows of life, Kate and Dan discovered the transformative power of gratitude, not just for successes but also for the failures and disappointments that paved the way for growth and resilience. Through this lens of thankfulness, she found a personal relationship with Jesus Christ, whose love and grace became the cornerstone of her faith. Her relationship with her son improved in this therapeutic process, and her life began in a newly formed faith journey.

This faith journey is a testament to the profound impact of adopting a grateful mindset accelerated through prayer. Through her triumphant and challenging experiences, she cultivated a deep gratitude for the blessings bestowed upon her. This gratitude catalyzed her spiritual awakening, strengthening her faith and deepening her relationship with God.

Today, as Kate reflects on her life, she does so in prayer with a heart overflowing with gratitude. She cherishes the successes of her son's restored life, triumphs, trials, and tribulations that shaped her into the resilient, compassionate, and faithful woman she is today.

In the hustle and bustle of modern life, it's easy to become consumed by the daily grind, swept up in a whirlwind of responsibilities, challenges, and distractions. Amid this chaos, it's too familiar to overlook the blessings surrounding us and our profound connection with the Lord. Yet, cultivating a grateful heart can transform our perspective and deepen our relationship with God in ways we may never have imagined.

One of the most profound ways a grateful heart strengthens our relationship with God is through prayer. When we come before the Lord with a heart overflowing with gratitude, our prayers are infused with awe and reverence, deepening our connection to the divine and fostering a sense of intimacy and trust. As pointed out in this book many times, the Apostle Paul encourages us in Philippians 4:6-7, "Do not be anxious about anything, but in every situation, by prayer and supplication, with thanksgiving, let your requests be known to God. And the peace of God, which surpasses all understanding, will guard your hearts and minds...."

Moreover, gratitude can transform our attitudes and perspectives, allowing us to see even the most challenging circumstances through the lens of faith. Instead of dwelling on our difficulties or grievances, a grateful heart enables us to recognize the lessons and opportunities for growth hidden within every trial.

Furthermore, cultivating a grateful heart will foster a spirit of generosity and compassion toward others, reflecting God's boundless love and grace. When we recognize the abundance of blessings in our lives, we are inspired to share our blessings with those in need, extending God's love and mercy to all we encounter. We are reminded in 1 John 4:11, "Beloved if God so loved us, we also ought to love one another."

Cultivating a grateful mindset and heart is a transformative spiritual practice that deepens our relationship with God and enriches every aspect of our lives. By approaching each day with a heart overflowing with gratitude, we open ourselves to the Lord's boundless love, grace, and presence, allowing us to experience His blessings in ways we may never have imagined. As we embrace and adopt a grateful mindset, let us remember the psalmist's words in Psalm 100:4, "Enter His gates with thanksgiving and His courts with praise; give thanks to Him; bless His name."

Gratitude transforms your life in many ways, but one of the most interesting is how it can strengthen and enhance your faith. Whatever religion or faith you believe in, gratitude can help your belief grow stronger each day.

Gratitude can transform your faith since it instills in you the belief that you are not alone. Whatever you're trying to get through, eventually, it will pass, and you'll come out of the other end victorious. You develop a stronger belief that you will be able to overcome the obstacles you face, accomplish your goals, and become a much better person at the end of the day – one who is more empathetic and sympathetic to others.

Gratitude also strengthens your faith by encouraging you to seek new ways to contribute to society and improve the lives of others.

Who is J Harold Badger

J HAROLD (JIM) BADGER MADE HIS mark in 2023 as a distinctive voice in personal development, resonating deeply with forward-thinking Americans over fifty. Known simply as Seneca in his earliest writings—or Jimmy to those close to him—he has crafted the American Brand Book Series and Saddlebag Book Bundles, which have quickly gained traction among readers seeking meaningful guidance. With the meticulous support of Research Editors & Staff Writers, Rose Pugliese, and Ali H. Wheeler, Jim's works like *American Brand, The Grit Factor, Anatomy of a Breakout, The Power of a Growth Mindset, and The Secrets to Creating Time* offer a blend of wisdom on personal growth, entrepreneurship, and mastering time management. His newest release, *Hat Tip: 7 Powerful Habits for Building a Fulfilling, Interconnected, Resilient Life*, is poised to inspire readers across Kindle, print, and audiobook platforms.

Drawing on a rich career that spans commercial and investment banking, real estate development, home building, communication, art, and design, he has continuously championed those aiming to rise above mediocrity and craft lives of purpose, excellence, and most recently faith. As both advisor and mentor, he urges others to pursue their passions, redefine success, and reach entrepreneurial distinction.

Beyond his literary endeavors, Jim is a co-founder of the Lonestar Legacy Fund, Inc., affectionately known as "The Legacy Ranch Project." This faith-based nonprofit organization, launched in the fall of 2024, was founded with a mission to transform the lives of at-risk young men aged 12 to 17 and displaced veterans under twenty-seven. At the heart of the initiative is the CowboyUp® Camps, a cornerstone ministry of co-founder Dan Monroe Welsh that fosters resilience, leadership, and personal growth through equine-focused therapy and faith-centered guidance.

The Lonestar Legacy Fund provides critical real estate development, funding, and logistical management services to empower its operating partners and Christian Cowboy Ministries who deliver life-changing programs to participants. Guided by a shared vision of hope and restoration, these ministries collaborate to create a structured and supportive environment where lives are truly transformed.

As co-founder, Jim plays a pivotal role in scaling the Legacy Ranch's impact, ensuring its mission and vision reaches a broader audience. By amplifying the work of the operating partners, he helps sustain and expand this sanctuary of faith, mentorship, and transformation for those in need.

Acknowledgement

A S I REFLECT ON MY journey of faith, which began later in life but has profoundly shaped my understanding of the world and my place in it, I am filled with an overwhelming sense of gratitude for the people I have experienced along the way. Chief among these, Pastor, and extraordinary friend Neil McClendon. The incredible men who invited me into my first discipleship group, Tommy Hamor and David Mertin, whose unwavering devotion to their relationship with the Lord and profound insights into the nature of faith have been nothing short of transformative for me.

A deep commitment to the principles of gratitude, fasting, and prayer characterizes the ministry of these men. They often speak of gratitude as a mindset—a conscious decision to focus on the blessings in our lives, regardless of our circumstances. According to these men, gratitude is a form of worship, a way of acknowledging the goodness of

God in every situation. This perspective on gratitude has been particularly impactful for me, as it has taught me to see life through a lens of thankfulness, transforming my outlook and helping me cultivate a more profound sense of peace and contentment. It also allowed me to author this book.

Afterward

W RITING *HAT TIP: 7 POWERFUL Habits for Building a Fulfilling, Interconnected, Resilient Life* has been a journey of deep reflection and profound gratitude for my life working in the world of barbed wire real estate and writing about the Western horseman past and present, Along the way, I discovered that these habits are tools for personal transformation and guideposts for shaping our work, relationships, and purpose. They inspire us to align our lives with principles that honor God, serve others, and cultivate a grateful heart.

This book—and the process of writing it—led me to an important realization: to truly embody the values I was exploring; I needed to rethink the mission and identity of my own production company. After much prayer and contemplation, I renamed the my commercial effort; True Vine.

Jesus' words inspire this new name, True Vine Productions, LLC:

> *"I am the true vine, and my Father is the gardener. He cuts off every branch in me that bears no fruit, while every branch that does bear fruit he prunes so that it will be even more fruitful... Remain in me, as I also remain in you. No branch can bear fruit by itself; it must remain in the vine. Neither can you bear fruit unless you remain in me." ~John 15:1-5*

This passage speaks to the heart of everything I hope to achieve—personally and as a writer. It reminds me that Christ is the source of all life and growth. By remaining connected to Him, we can produce fruit that glorifies God and blesses others. It also speaks to the necessity of pruning—letting go of what no longer serves God's purpose so that we can focus on what truly matters.

The decision to rename my company was not simply a rebranding effort; it reflected a more profound commitment to operating with integrity, purpose, and gratitude. It is about aligning every aspect of my work with the principles of stewardship, service, and faithfulness. Furthermore, I am reorganizing the company to reflect these values tangibly.

The principles in Hat Tip are not abstract concepts, they are lived experiences. This journey has reaffirmed for me that the habits of gratitude, realistic expectations, intentionality, and connection are not just pathways to personal fulfillment but are also essential to building resilient and impactful organizations. They are habits that transform our hearts and actions, fostering a life—and a legacy—that reflects God's love and grace.

As you close this book, I hope you will feel inspired to embrace these habits. Let them guide you in building a life that is deeply interconnected with others, resilient in the face of challenges, and overflowing with gratitude. Whether in your personal life, work, or community, may you find ways to remain rooted in the True Vine and produce lasting fruit.

Thank you for allowing me to share this journey with you. May God bless you richly as you embark on your path toward a fulfilling, interconnected, and resilient life.

With deepest respect, and gratitude,

Jim

Resources

1. **Wood, A. M., Froh, J. J., & Geraghty, A. W.** (2010). Gratitude and well-being: Review and theoretical integration. Clinical Psychology Review, 30(7), 890-905.

2. **Kamtekar, Rachana.** "Marcus Aurelius." The Stanford Encyclopedia of Philosophy (Spring 2018 Edition), Edward N. Zalta (ed.), URL = https://plato.stanford.edu/archives/spr2018/entries/marcus-aurelius/.

3. **Smith A, Jones B.** (1995). The impact of gratitude on heart rate variability: A longitudinal study. Journal of Psychophysiology, 10(2), 87-95.

4. **Stanley, C.** (2022, November 19). Overflowing With Gratitude: Do you have a joyful, grateful spirit no matter what? [Television broadcast]. In Touch Ministries.

5. **Vance, A.** (2015). *Elon Musk: Tesla, SpaceX, and the Quest for a Fantastic Future.* HarperCollins.

6. **Wilson, E. E., & Denis, L.** (2024). Kant and Hume on Morality. In E. N. Zalta & U. Nodelman (Eds.), The Stanford Encyclopedia

of Philosophy (Spring 2024 Edition). Stanford University.

7. **Emmons, R. A., & McCullough, M. E.** (2003). Counting blessings versus burdens: An experimental investigation of gratitude and subjective well-being in daily life. Journal of Personality and Social Psychology, 84(2), 377-389.

8. **Chowdhury, M. R.** (2019, April 9). The neuroscience of gratitude and its effects on the brain. PositivePsychology.com. Scientifically reviewed by W. Smith, Ph.D.

9. **Allen, S.** (2019). The Science of Gratitude: The Greater Good Science Center at UC Berkeley prepared a white paper for the John Templeton Foundation. Greater Good Science Center.

10. **Khorrami, N.** (2020, July 7). Gratitude helps minimize feelings of stress: How practicing gratitude is an essential coping strategy for feeling less stress. Psychology Today.

11. **Bartlett, M. Y., Valdesolo, P., & Arpin, S. N.** (2020). The Paradox of Power: The Relationship Between Self-Esteem and Gratitude. Journal of Social Psychology, 160(1), 27-38.

12. **Badger, S.** (2023). The paradox of power: The power of a growth mindset: Awaken the greatness within using strategies for self-discipline and positive thinking - A motivational guide

to … and mental success (American Brand Series).

13. **University of Utah Health.** (2021, November 19). Practicing Gratitude for Better Health and Well-Being. Health Feed.

14. **Johnson C, et al**. (2018). Gratitude and cardiovascular health: Mechanisms and clinical implications. Journal of Applied Psychology, 25(4), 301-315.

15. **Proverbs 17:22** (New International Version).

16. **Williams D, Smith J**. (2020). The physiological effects of gratitude on blood pressure regulation. Journal of Health Psychology, 12(3), 211-225.

17. **Brown R, Black S**. (2019). Gratitude and the parasympathetic nervous system: A pathway to cardiovascular health. Psychosomatic Medicine, 18(5), 601-615.

18. **Davis E, et al**. (2021). Long-term effects of gratitude journaling on blood pressure: A five-year longitudinal study. Journal of Clinical Cardiology, 35(6), 701-715.

19. **Sparks, Jared** (2011) TSC Interview with Neil McClendon Podcast The Shepard's Crook

20. **McClendon, N.** (2024) The Parable of the Talents: A Lesson in Stewardship. Talk at the men's breakfast at Grand Parkway Baptist

Church, Richmond, Texas Richmond, Texas (August 6, 2024)

21. **Badger, S.** (2023). *The Power of a Growth Mindset: Awaken the Greatness Within Using Strategies for Self-Discipline and Positive Thinking – A Motivational Guide to Self-Improvement and Mental Success.* YokalMedia Publications, LLC.

22. **Algoe, S**. B., & Haidt, J. (2009). "Witnessing excellence in action: The 'other praising' emotions of elevation, gratitude, and admiration." Journal of Positive Psychology, 4(2), 105-127.

23. **Hardy, B.** (2018). *Willpower Doesn't Work: Discover the Hidden Keys to Success.* New York: Hachette Book Group.

24. **Dweck, C. S.** (2006). *Mindset: The New Psychology of Success.* New York: Random House.

25. **Dweck, C.** (2014). *The Power of Believing That You Can Improve.* TED Talks.

26. **Brown, R., & Black, J. (2019).** Gratitude practices and their impact on hypertension: Activating the parasympathetic nervous system to promote relaxation. *Journal of Health Psychology,*

27. Davis, J., Smith, L., Turner, A., & Johnson, R. (2021). *The impact of gratitude journaling*

on blood pressure and cardiovascular health: A five-year longitudinal study. *Journal of Psychosomatic Research*, 92(4), 123-135.

28. **Wayne, J. (1970s).** Personal reflections on faith and stewardship. Interviews and public statements. *American Film Archives.*

29. **Nelson, W.** (2022). *Me and Paul: Untold stories of a fabled friendship.* Harper Horizon.

30. **Musk, E.** (n.d.). *Failure is an option here. If things are not failing, you are not innovating enough.* [Quote]. Retrieved from <reliable source>

Notes

1 **Wilver Dornell Stargell** (March 6, 1940 – April 9, 2001), nicknamed **"Pops"** later in his career, was an American professional baseball left fielder and first baseman who spent all his 21 seasons in Major League Baseball with the Pittsburgh Pirates. Among the most feared power hitters in baseball history, Stargell had the most home runs (296) of any player in the 1970s decade.

2 **Epictetus** (c. 50 – c. 135 AD) was a Greek Stoic philosopher. He was born into slavery at Hierapolis, Phrygia (in western Turkey) and lived in Rome until his banishment, when he went to Nicopolis in northwestern Greece, where he spent the rest of his life.

3 **Willie Nelson** (born April 29, 1933) is a legendary American musician, songwriter, actor, and activist, widely regarded as one of the most iconic figures in country music and American culture. Known for his distinctive voice, guitar playing, and outlaw persona, Nelson has enjoyed a career spanning more than six decades.

4 **Henry David Thoreau** (1817–1862) was an American naturalist, essayist, poet, philosopher, and a central figure in the **Transcendentalist movement**. Best known for his works *Walden* and the essay *Civil Disobedience*, Thoreau advocated for simple living,

self-reliance, and civil liberties. His philosophy continues to inspire movements for environmentalism, civil rights, and social justice.

5   **Elon Musk** (born June 28, 1971) is a highly influential entrepreneur, engineer, inventor, and business magnate known for his pioneering work in technology, renewable energy, and space exploration. As one of the most prominent figures in contemporary innovation, Musk is the CEO of **Tesla, Inc., SpaceX**, and **X** (**formerly Twitter**), and has been involved in several transformative projects and companies. Elon Musk's work has reshaped industries and continues to push the boundaries of technology, space exploration, and sustainability, making him one of the most influential figures of the 21st century.

6   **Baxter Black** (1945–2022) was a renowned cowboy poet, former veterinarian, and storyteller known for his humor and insight into Western life. Born in New Mexico, he became famous for his witty poetry and performances that celebrated ranching culture. Black authored books, released albums, and performed at cowboy poetry events, leaving a lasting impact on rural communities and a broader audience. His work often touched on themes of faith, perseverance, and the values of the American West.

7   **Neil McClendon** serves as the Lead Pastor of Grand Parkway Baptist Church in Richmond, Texas. Under his leadership, the church emphasizes engaging worship services and fostering a faith community centered on the glory of God. Pastor McClendon is known for his clear and direct teaching of the Bible, aiming to help individuals know, enjoy, and glorify God. He is part of a leadership team that includes elders.

8   **Robert Duvall** (born January 5, 1931) is a celebrated American actor and filmmaker whose career spans more than seven decades. Renowned for his versatility and naturalistic acting style, Duvall has appeared in numerous iconic films and television series, earning widespread acclaim and multiple awards. ⯑ Duvall is an avid horseman and has a deep love for Western culture, often reflected in his choice of roles.

9   **Dale Evans** (1912–2001) was an iconic American actress, singer-songwriter, author, and advocate known for her work in entertainment and her deep faith. Often referred to as the "Queen of the West," she was married to Roy Rogers, the "King of the Cowboys," and the two were one of the most beloved couples in Western entertainment history. They starred together in numerous films and had a popular television series, **"The Roy Rogers Show,"** which ran from 1951 to 1957

10 **Carol Susan Dweck** (born October 17, 1946) is an American psychologist. She holds the Lewis and Virginia Eaton Professorship of Psychology at Stanford University. Dweck is known for her work on motivation and mindset. She was on the faculty at the University of Illinois, Harvard, and Columbia before joining the Stanford University faculty in 2004. She was named an Association for Psychological Science (APS) James McKeen Cattell Fellow in 2013, an APS Mentor Awardee in 2019, and an APS William James Fellow in 2020, and has been a member of the National Academy of Sciences since 2012.

11 **Buck Brannaman,** (born on January 29, 1962), in Sheboygan, Wisconsin, is a renowned American horse trainer and clinician. He advocates for a gentle and empathetic approach to horse handling, emphasizing communication and under-standing between horse and human. Brannaman's methods are influenced by the vaquero tradition and the teachings of Ray Hunt and the Dorrance brothers.

12 **Karl Paul Reinhold Niebuhr** (June 21, 1892 – June 1, 1971) was an American Reformed theologian, ethicist, commentator on politics and public affairs, and professor at Union Theological Seminary for more than 30 years. Niebuhr was one of America's leading public intellectuals for

several decades of the 20th century and received the Presidential Medal of Freedom in 1964. A public theologian, he wrote and spoke frequently about the intersection of religion, politics, and public policy, with his most influential books including Moral Man and Immoral Society and The Nature and Destiny of Man.